$\int f \mathbf{P}$

Also by Shelby Steele

*White Guilt:*
*How Blacks and Whites Together*
*Destroyed the Promise of the Civil Rights Era*

*A Dream Deferred:*
*The Second Betrayal of Black Freedom*
*in America*

*The Content of Our Character:*
*A New Vision of Race in America*

# A Bound Man

WHY WE ARE EXCITED ABOUT OBAMA
AND WHY HE CAN'T WIN

Shelby Steele

FREE PRESS

New York   London   Toronto   Sydney

FREE PRESS

A Division of Simon & Schuster, Inc.
1230 Avenue of the Americas
New York, NY 10020

First Free Press hardcover edition January 2008

FREE PRESS and colophon are trademarks of Simon & Schuster, Inc.

For information about special discounts for bulk purchases,
please contact Simon & Schuster Special Sales at 1-800-456-6798
or  business@simonandschuster.com

DESIGNED BY ERICH HOBBING

Manufactured in the United States of America

10   9   8   7   6   5   4   3   2   1

Library of Congress Cataloging-in-Publication Data
Steele, Shelby.
A bound man: why we are excited about Obama and why he can't win /
Shelby Steele.
p.  cm.
1. Obama, Barack.   2. Obama, Barack—Public opinion.
3. African Americans—Public opinion.   4. Presidential candidates—
United States.   5. Presidents—United States—Election—2008.
6. United States—Politics and government—2001–.   7. United States—
Race relations—Political aspects.   8. Public opinion—United States.   I. Title.
E901.1.023S74   2008
328.73092—dc22                    2007031711

ISBN-13:  978-1-4165-5917-7
ISBN-10:      1-4165-5917-5

*To Rita, my partner in thought*

# CONTENTS

## Part I: The Man

## Part II: The Society

CONTENTS

# A Bound Man

WHY WE ARE EXCITED ABOUT OBAMA
AND WHY HE CAN'T WIN

PART I

# The Man

# CHAPTER ONE

# The High Possibility

The first thing I ever heard about Barack Obama was that he had a white mother and a black father. Interestingly, the person who informed me of this spoke only matter-of-factly, with no hint of the gossip's wicked delight. Yet this piece of information was presented as vital, as one of those all-important facts about a person that, like the first cause of a complex truth, plays a role in everything that follows. Apparently, it is Barack Obama's fate to have notice of his racial pedigree precede even the mention of his politics—as if the pedigree inevitably explains the politics. And I suspect that some people would feel a bit defrauded were they to hear his political ideas and only later learn that he was racially mixed.

Of course, I am rather sensitive to all this because I,

too, was born to a white mother and a black father, though I did not fully absorb this fact, which would have been so obvious to the outside world, until I was old enough to notice the world's fascination—if not obsession—with it. To this day it is all but impossible for me to actually stop and think of my parents as white and black or to think of myself, therefore, as half and half. This is the dumb mathematics of thinking by race— dumb because race is used here as a kind of bullying truth that pushes aside actual human experience. So I never know what people really want to know when they ask me what it is like to be—and here come the math words—"biracial" or "multiracial" or "multicultural." The self as the answer to an addition problem.

But, as best as I can surmise, what people really want to know is what it is like to have no race to go home to at night. We commonly think of race as a kind of home, a place where they have to take you in; and it seems the very stuff of alienation to live without solid footing in such a home. If this alienation is not nearly as dramatic as the old "tragic mulatto" stories would suggest, it nevertheless does exist. How could it not in a society like America where race once meant the difference between slavery and freedom? Racist societies enforce the idea of race as home by making race an inescapable fate. So, still today, this fundamentally odd—even primitive—idea remains embedded in our democratic national culture, the legacy of our past. People who are the progeny of two races have a more ambiguous racial fate and, therefore, at least some feeling of homelessness. They stand just outside the reach of that automatic racial solidarity that those born of one race can take for granted.

So, people like Barack Obama and me are always under a degree of suspicion. The "one drop" rule formulated in the days of slavery—one drop of black blood makes you black—consigns us to the black race (happily so for me and, I would imagine, for Obama as well), but the fact of an immediate white parent differentiates us and interrupts solidarity with blacks. And all this is worsened by the fact that whites are historically the "oppressor" race. Thus, by the dumb logic of racial thinking, our very mother's milk comes through a collaboration with the enemy. More literally, this "collaboration" may mean that we enjoy more exposure to the dominant culture, more advantages in a color-conscious society. Mistrust and even resentment from other blacks often ensues. And from whites come the sneers one commonly hears in reference to Obama—"he's not even really black."

Our vulnerability is that both blacks and whites can use our impossible racial authenticity against us. Both races can throw up our mixed background to challenge our authority to speak. And both races can squeeze us in a blueslike double bind where the absurdity is as comic as it is tragic: we dismiss you for not being authentically black, yet we will never accept you as authentically black. Ha ha. When people can call you inauthentic and undermine your moral authority, they have a degree of power in relation to you. And where they have power, you have vulnerability.

This would have to be an old and tiresome vulnerability in Barack Obama's life (as it is in mine), and all the more so because he has chosen a public life. One senses that his first book, *Dreams from My Father,* was meant in part to diffuse some of this vulnerability. In it he does not merely "own up" to his interracial background as if to a past indiscretion; he candidly explores it. He practices that brave and aggressive self-disclosure that disarms by taking away the gossip's ability to surprise. It is harder to deploy a man's vulnerability against him when he publishes it in a book.

Still, I glimpsed some of the weariness he must feel at having this vulnerability regularly probed in a *60 Minutes* interview that aired near the launching of his presidential campaign. It was the usual *60 Minutes* setup, the camera in close enough for a dermatological exam. And there sat Obama, perfectly composed and seemingly ready for anything, the now famous ears framing his good looks in eternal boyishness. The correspondent, Steve Kroft, asked a series of predictable political questions and then, hunching forward a bit, entered the territory of identity. There was an allusion to the mixed-race background, and a question about how Obama saw himself. And here—probably because I knew so well what to look for—I saw the very faintest exasperation come into his eyes and then instantly vanish. Barack Obama has no doubt had a lifetime of rehearsals for this moment, and he must have had a hundred answers immediately at hand, all rehearsed to the point of glibness. Yet the answer he finally gave had real pathos precisely because it was so glib.

He was "rooted," he said, in the African-American community, but he was also "more than that." To be sure, this is the formulation of a man with a very complex identity trying, understandably, to make himself simpler and more recognizable to a society not used to pondering his like. Yet, this is also a formulation that reduces Obama's identity to a banality. What could "rooted" or "more than that" mean? How would the two be simultaneously possible? And, for that matter, what could "African-American community" really mean? A culture? A politics? To become recognizable, he processes himself through the same dumb racial math—he is one thing plus something else—that has been the very source of his vulnerability. He collaborates with the same tired racial conventions that made him an odd man out to begin with.

And yet a great part of Obama's appeal in broader America—especially his political appeal—can be chalked up to his complex identity. He is interesting for not fitting into old racial conventions. Not only does he stand in stark contrast to a black leadership with which Americans of all races have grown exhausted—the likes of Al

Sharpton, Jesse Jackson, and Julian Bond—he embodies something that no other presidential candidate possibly can: the idealism that race is but a negligible human difference. Here is the radicalism, innate to his pedigree, that automatically casts him as the perfect antidote to America's corrosive racial politics. After all, this is the radicalism by which Martin Luther King put Americans in touch—if only briefly—with their human universality. Barack Obama is the progeny of this idealism. And, as such, he is a living rebuke to both racism and racialism, to both segregation and identity politics—to any form of collective chauvinism. For all his misfittedness, he also embodies a great and noble human aspiration: to smother racial power in a democracy of individuals. To stand in the glow of so high an aspiration is to seem a bit enchanted or, at the very least, charismatic.

It doesn't matter that he sometimes goes along with race-based policies, or that he made his own Faustian bargain with affirmative action (no college-bound black of his generation could avoid this self-compromise). No one is excited because Obama nods to identity politics; people are excited because he *represents* an idealism that opposes such politics. Any black who takes on the near-absolute visibility that goes with seeking such high office will function as both a man and a symbol, and sometimes the two will be at odds. So it is not surprising that Obama the man may vary a bit from Obama the symbol.

And, as a symbol, he raises several remarkable possibilities. Is America now the kind of society that can allow a black—of whatever pedigree—to become the most powerful human being on earth, the commander of the greatest military in history? Have our democratic principles at last moved us beyond even the tribalism of race? And will the black American identity, still so reflexively focused on victimization, be nullified if a black wins the presidency of this largely white nation?

The cultural and historical implications of Obama's candidacy are clearly greater than its public policy implications. While Obama the man labors in the same political vineyard as his competitors, mapping out policy positions on everything from war to health care, his candidacy itself asks the American democracy to virtually complete itself, to achieve that almost perfect transparency where color is indeed no veil over character— where a black, like a white, can put himself forward as the individual he truly is. This is the aspirational significance of Obama's campaign, the high possibility that it points to quite apart from its policy goals.

CHAPTER TWO

# Plausibility

But whether or not Obama's presidential campaign gains this high ground, it has already achieved historical significance. And this achievement is simply the plausibility of Barack Obama as a presidential candidate. It is conceivable that this black man could be voted into the presidency of the United States by a broad and multiracial swath of the American electorate, if not in this current election season, then in a subsequent one.

This possibility became plausible, despite America's tortured racial history, for two reasons. The first is that white America, since the sixties, has undergone a moral evolution away from racism so transformative that there is now something like a desire in the body politic to see a truly qualified black person in the White House. Of course, this desire may be only ephemeral goodwill, as wistful as it is unexamined. It may be only a kind of fatalism, a desire to have over with some difficult inevitability. Nevertheless, there is now openness to a prospect that was inconceivable only a short time ago. If nothing else, Barack Obama's sudden and broad popularity verifies the presence of this new openness for the first time. When you can credibly run for the presidency only two years out of the Illinois state legislature and, upon announcing your campaign, immediately surge past all but one competitor, then something in society is drawing you forward.

The second thing that makes Obama's candidacy plausible is, of course, Obama himself. To begin with, he is blessed with remarkable political talent. It is no accident that the word "Kennedyesque" so often trails in his wake. He is tall, elegant as well as eloquent, and seemingly comfortable in his own skin. He orates movingly and writes with the narrative skill of a novelist. With so much natural facility, he could easily have nurtured a Clintonesque slickness. But Obama's weaknesses stem from earnestness more than glibness. He hasn't yet mastered the humorous or ironic quip, and he can sometimes be inadvertently elitist—rearing back and calling an enemy a Social Darwinist, as if to devastate him. His passions seem more of the head than of the heart, and, clearly, he would be a far more cerebral president than America is used to.

After announcing his own bid for the Democratic

nomination last winter, Senator Joseph Biden made the innocuously racist comment that Obama was "articulate, bright, and clean." This was racist because it celebrated Obama at the expense of other blacks who were presumably inarticulate, not bright, and unclean. Also, it showed surprise at high ability in a black. Senator Biden's words, for all their unfortunate double entendre, represented a common response to Obama: that this young man is surprising because he is both black and apparently quite able. He seems to meet, and possibly exceed, the basic ability bar for people seeking such high office, white or black.

And in Obama's case this bar is very specific. His abilities can never be seen to depend on the condescensions of white guilt. As a black, Obama must display enough natural talent to be immune to the stigma of affirmative action—the perception that he is a mediocrity lifted up by the lowered standards that so many American institutions have strewn in the path of college-bound and college-educated blacks for decades. Affirmative action has become a stigma of minority inferiority in American life. Even in highest officialdom, affirmative action is rationalized by viewing blacks as almost interminably weak—as a race that will need racial preferences for at least another quarter century (this according to Justice Sandra Day O'Connor in the 2003 University of Michigan affirmative action case). Obama must make sure to separate himself from this pitying stigma, from his race's reputation for weakness, in order to achieve plausibility as a presidential candidate.

Still, he has clearly benefited from affirmative action. American universities impose this policy on black students with such totalitarian resolve that even blacks who don't need the lowered standards come away stigmatized by them. What began to separate Obama from this stigma was his editorship of the *Harvard Law Review.* Here was something that required genuine merit. Here was a position that he had to gain through competition rather than through the suspension of competition. Obama's fame began precisely with this achievement because it distinguished him from the general run of black students who carried the stigma (even if not true) of having been pulled forward by lowered standards. He was *special* because he was clearly more than an "affirmative action baby," someone who could succeed without the ministrations of white guilt.

Obama is "fresh," Senator Biden said by way of apology the day after his faux pas. And here again he was right. Blacks like Obama, who show merit where mediocrity is expected, enjoy a kind of reverse stigma, a slightly inflated reputation for "freshness" and excellence simply because they defy expectations. Add to this, in Obama's case, a thoughtful and beautifully written first book (the contract for which came out of the excitement around his law review editorship), and the reputation becomes almost an aura.

The point is that Obama has separated himself from the deadly stigmas of black inferiority and white paternalism. He is seen as untainted by the former and in no need of the latter. This does not mean that people won't consider his race in some way as they ponder his candidacy. It only means that they can consider his candidacy without feeling guilted, intimidated, or otherwise manipulated by his race. And this is what makes him the first *plausible* black presidential candidate in American history.

# CHAPTER THREE

# Search for the Father

And yet, the issue of race—so nicely contained and deactivated in the Barack Obama political persona—is still very much alive within the man himself. The black identity —with the claustrophobic politics and militant sensibilities of its post-sixties incarnation—has been nearly a lifelong preoccupation for Obama. By the surface facts of his life—the mixed-raced background, the childhood in Hawaii and Indonesia—it would be easy to assume, as many have, that he might be indifferent to the whole business of race and identity. There is a tendency to see Obama as a kind of "new man," someone spared the intractable fates of being simply black or white in America. Out of an understandable race fatigue, many Americans want to believe that there are people on whom race sits very lightly, people whose very hybridism suggests the possibility of transcending race.

But Barack Obama is not such a person. His books show a man nothing less than driven by a determination to be black, as if blackness were more an achievement than a birthright. And this need within him, as understandable as it might be, puts Obama at odds with himself. His plausibility as a candidate comes, in part, from the perception that he is not driven to be black, that he is rather lightly tethered to his race. But rhe very arc of his life—from Hawaii to the South Side of Chicago—has been greatly influenced by an often conscious resolve to "belong" irrefutably to the black identity.

Where does such resolve come from? What sort of alienation drives it? In Obama's case, the answer seems to begin far away from race, in a much more mundane circumstance: his relationship to his father.

If there is a single archetypal theme that animates Barack Obama's early life, it would have to be "the search for the father." Of course, there is something of this quest in everyone's life. Some sort of coming to terms with the father—or surrogate father—is one of the ways human beings, consciously and unconsciously, construct their personalities.

In literature, the search for the father always follows a similar pattern. A charming example is Nathaniel

Hawthorne's story "My Kinsman, Major Molineaux," in which a young man leaves his village for the city in the conviction that he will find there his prosperous uncle (surrogate father) who will provide for him and set him up in business. His uncle, he knows, is a big man in the city, so when the young man arrives unfortuitously in the middle of the night, he stops people on the street and proudly asks them if they know where he can find "my kinsman, Major Molineaux." Many small adventures and humiliations follow, yet the young man keeps his faith, knowing within himself that his uncle is an important man and that all will be well as soon as he finds him. Then, in the deep of night, as he is standing on a street, a little lost, he notices in the distance an angry crowd coming his way. More than anything else, he feels the country boy's curiosity at what might be going on. As the crowd draws nearer he sees that they have tarred and feathered a man and are about the business of running him out of town on a rail. The young man is just beginning to absorb this "big city" happening when the crowd finally passes directly in front of him. And this is when he sees very clearly that the man hanging from the rail is his uncle, Major Molineaux.

Search-for-the-father stories always begin in the perfectly normal childhood illusion that the father will always do two things: provide for our basic needs and interpret for us the frightening world outside the family. Another part of this illusion is the irrepressible feeling that these things—shelter and meaning—are our birthright and our father's preordained obligation. At the core of this archetype is the childish, but quite real, longing for the father to have a magic that spares us conflict, struggle, doubt, and anxiety. The young man in the Hawthorne story comes to the city unannounced but with a perfect faith that his well-off uncle will provide for him and show him how to make his way. He believes this is his birthright, something he can take for granted. So he is wrapped in a perfectly innocent peace.

And then comes the inevitable existential shock, the crash of events that strip away all illusion. Suddenly there is absolutely nothing between him and the wild world, no shelter, no received wisdom to point the way, nothing. The search-for-the-father always ends in this kind of initiation. We look up and see that the father, for all the magic we have assigned to him, is merely human and limited, incapable of saving us even if he wanted to. Falling from illusion to reality, we get nothing of what we had hoped for; we get only an epiphany: we are alone, and our manhood or womanhood requires that we stand alone and learn to interpret the world for ourselves.

In literature, archetypal themes are often overstated a bit to make the case. Still, if only metaphorically, they point to eternal truths. We do search for the father, for shelter and meaning that can simply be received from a paternal authority. And many of us have fathers who, while never achieving the perfection our childish heart may long for, do an extraordinary job of both sheltering and interpreting. I was blessed to have such a father. And yet I learned very early that there were traumas he could not protect me from and answers that he did not have. I am quite sure today that my own life—the life that follows, for better and for worse, from my own making— began with the intuition that my father could not rescue me from the most serious blows I endured as a youth. Of course he couldn't; no father can. And so, emotionally, I learned what it was like to be alone. But then I also began to feel a certain excitement at the autonomy and self-possession this opened to me. The loss of that illusionary all-knowing father was also the opportunity to make my own life.

Barack Obama's first book, *Dreams from My Father*, chronicles his search for his father, and it is especially poignant because his father left the family when Barack was only two and, except for one brief visit when Barack was ten, never returned. Superficial logic might suggest that an absent father would spare the child all the illusions involved in the search-for-the-father. But of course, the opposite is true. When the father is not there, he usually becomes larger than life, an image assembled out of longing and imagination. He often becomes the idealized father that everyone wants but that no one gets. As such, he necessarily becomes an obsession in ways that real and present fathers never do. But there will also be an ongoing sense of injustice, of being cheated, because

21

the father's absence is also a denial of birthright. Worse, it is a kind of rejection. So one longs for him and resents him at the same time.

Barack Obama's fall from illusion to reality came on the night he met his older sister, Auma, for the first time. She is their father's daughter by his first African wife and, on her first night in Barack's tiny Chicago apartment, she describes their father as he really was. And the man Barack had always pictured as a formidable patriarch emerges as a figure of pathos, a man of some talent beset by petty weaknesses and the sort of arrogance that covers an inner faithlessness. Barack writes:

> I felt as if my world had been turned on its head; as if I had woken up to find a blue sun in the yellow sky. . . . All my life I had carried a single image of my father. . . . The brilliant scholar, the generous friend, the upstanding leader—my father had been all those things. All those things and more, because except for that one brief visit in Hawaii, he had never been present to foil that image, because I hadn't seen what perhaps most men see at some point in their lives: their father's body shrinking, their father's best hopes dashed, their father's face lined with grief and regret.

Barack's father had created several families in Africa and America, and then left them. He supported some children spottily, others not at all. But he managed to mark all his children with abandonment. He ruined a promising career in government through arrogance and inflexibility, and then watched his lessers rise above him. More and more, he turned to drink.

On that night in Chicago, Barack saw his father tarred, feathered, and hanging from a rail.

> Now, as I sat in the glow of a single light bulb, rocking slightly on a hard-backed chair, [the inflated image of his father] vanished. Replaced by . . . what? A bitter drunk? An abusive husband? A defeated, lonely bureaucrat? To think that all my life I had been wrestling with nothing more than a ghost!

And then the epiphany:

> The king is overthrown, I thought. The emerald curtain is pulled aside. . . . I can do what I damn well please. For what man, if not my father, has the power to tell me otherwise? Whatever I do, it seems, I won't do much worse than he did.

Reading Obama's moving account of that long-ago Chicago night—his sister asleep on the fold-out couch, him rocking back and forth in a straight-backed chair under a single light bulb—one can only cheer for him.

What an extraordinary liberation to achieve after so many years. Yes, his fall into reality leaves him alone, but even so, the company is better. And there is the consolation of a surprising irony: the father who gave him so little, in the end gave him the best gift a father can give: authority over his own life.

# CHAPTER FOUR

# Becoming an Authentic Black

Nevertheless, to find release from the actual father is not—necessarily—to be done wrestling with paternal authority. And to have lived so long in the void left by an absent father, to have gone through so much idealization and longing in one's most formative years, to have so insistently nurtured oneself on a chimera—well, this is how archetypes implant their forms within us. And these forms often remain to echo throughout our lives even after the vulnerability that originally caused them has been overcome.

Did Barack Obama's search for his real father simply fold into his search for a secure black identity? Was this identity a surrogate father, a more dependable manifestation of paternal authority? It is hard to go with a psychology this pat, in which the correspondences are so perfectly symmetrical: the father and the racial identity as neatly interchangeable objects of quest. It goes too far to argue that Obama sought racial identity in his father and a father in racial identity. Still, he comes close to saying just this. On that night, when the father of his imaginings crashes to earth, one of his most agonized cries has to do with identity:

> Yes, I'd seen weaknesses in other men . . . men I might love but never emulate, white men and brown men whose fates didn't speak to my own. It was into my father's image, the black man, son of Africa, that I'd packed all the attributes I sought in myself, the attributes of Martin and Malcolm, DuBois and Mandela. . . . [My] father's voice had . . . remained untainted, inspiring, rebuking, granting or withholding approval. You do not work hard enough, Barry. You must help in your people's struggle. Wake up, black man!

Yes, but wake up as a black man where? In his upscale private high school in Hawaii, where his "people's struggle" could have been no more than a textbook reference? At Columbia and Harvard universities, where minority students are so showered with opportunity that racial protest can only be theater? The black identity that Obama projects in this passage has the same feel of idealization and longing that his original vision of his father had. It, too, seems invented against the alienation of an absence. And in truth, with a white mother, the absent black father was also an absent black identity. So the references to "Martin and Malcolm," "your people's struggle," "Wake up, black man" idealize the absent black identity in the same way that "brilliant scholar," "generous friend," and "upstanding leader" idealized the absent father.

This is the circumstance, then, that makes the father and the black identity virtually interchangeable as objects of his personal search. The young Obama experienced both his father and his racial identity as absences, while most people enjoy these same things as birthrights. Not only does he have to search self-consciously for surrogate versions of what others take for granted but, as he puts his identity together in this way, he will likely be trailed by the feeling that he is jerrybuilt where others are naturally solid.

I know a little of this feeling myself. If I was blessed to have the clarity of a strong and present black father, my experience with the black identity was more ambiguous. I grew up in the last decades of segregation, when race was a hard determinism. For the impropriety of marrying a black man, my white mother was made to live as a black woman. I was born in a black maternity ward, grew up in a black community, and went to a segregated black school—pretty good credentials upon which to claim a black identity, if living out the oppressive fate of one's group is what nails down identity.

And yet, children of interracial unions often have their identities questioned the instant they are discovered to have a white parent. Though it is rarely said openly, the white parent is often seen as a stain of inauthenticity on the black identity by both blacks and whites. Worse, this inauthenticity sometimes generalizes beyond race to indict the entire personal character. When Barack Obama is called a "Halfrican," the point is not simply that he comes from a mixed-race background; it is also that he is a kind of phony, a pretender to blackness. For racially mixed blacks, the search for "authentic" blackness is also a search for *personal* credibility and legitimacy. Our era of intense identity politics means that such people live under a permanent accusation of inauthenticity. And they are consigned the Sisyphean labor of forever proving a negative: that they are not inauthentic.

Immediately after college I spent over three years working in Great Society social programs in what was arguably the poorest and most crime-ridden black city in America—East St. Louis, Illinois. Very soon after college, Barack Obama spent a similar number of years working as a community organizer in some of the poorest black neighborhoods on the South Side of Chicago. I am sure that youthful idealism was a strong motivation in my case and, very likely, in Obama's as well. Still, human motivation is always a mixed affair. And, on some level, I knew even then that I was also erecting a black identity. In East St. Louis, I was, among other things, searching for authenticity and legitimacy *as a black*.

This was the late sixties and early seventies, when the idea of a militant black identity—based on protest politics and a tight cultural/racial unity—took over black America. In the early civil rights era, it had been our universal humanity, not our blackness, that had made the case for our freedom. But after the civil rights victories of the mid-sixties, the movement for black advancement abruptly became an identity movement. Suddenly, our race, not our common humanity, was the agent of uplift. And "black power" was the new faith in identity as power.

All this came at me in my very early twenties, just before and during my East St. Louis years, and it cut straight to the core of my identity insecurity. On a landscape where blackness had emerged as an atavistic truth—a celebration of racial essentialism—I was suddenly standing in a territory of stark inauthenticity. After all, my mother came from upper (ever-so-slightly)-middle-class, small-town America (Jimmy Stewart territory), and qualified to be a Daughter of the American Revolution, though she would sooner have died than joined. And so I came to feel that there were only two options. I could reject "blackness" and the identity politics that accompanied it. Clearly, I did not really believe in "blackness." I thought it little more than a style of clenched fists, Afros, and right-on phrases. It sought redemption in what had been a mark of shame, but it had no relationship to accomplishment. Yet to reject it implied collaboration with white supremacy, the most disgraceful sort of Uncle Tomism. To avoid this horror, the second option was simply to pretend, to go along with blackness despite my true feelings.

In East St. Louis, I was still too much in need of authenticity to risk the first option. So I became immersed in an irony: I would pursue authenticity through pretense. I would go along with a "blackness" I did not really believe in so as to gain the acceptance I could claim as authenticity. I did not consciously do this, but this is what I did.

And, in fact, my mixed-race background was only an additional pressure toward this kind of duplicity. All blacks of my generation came under pressure to join the new militant identity. And many became immersed in the same irony—going along with an unexamined "blackness" simply to belong. Whenever collective identities become self-conscious, sharply defined, and highly politicized, people begin to survive them through duplicity. Still, for the mixed-race black, both the need to belong and the inability to believe are likely to be more pronounced. Racial "authenticity" will require even more duplicity and pretense.

The illusion is that such people are less encumbered by the black identity than others. And this may be true for those mixed-raced blacks who choose to distance themselves from the black identity. But for those who don't, this identity is more encumbering than for other blacks because it forces the personality to accommodate more blatant contradictions—acceptance of the racial categories in identity politics, for example, when one is in fact of two races. For the mixed-race black, today's highly politicized black identity is reachable only through a degree of self-betrayal.

CHAPTER FIVE

# Belonging

*. . . it remained necessary to prove which side you were on, to show your loyalty to the black masses . . .*

*The constant, crippling fear that I didn't belong somehow, that unless I dodged and hid and pretended to be something I wasn't I would forever remain an outsider, with the rest of the world, black and white, always standing in judgment . . .*

*Was that all that had brought me to Chicago, I wondered—the desire for such simple acceptance?*
                                    *—Dreams from My Father*

At one point during his days as a community organizer, Barack Obama had a conversation with a fellow organizer about how terrifying young black males had become. This is a staple conversation in and around inner cities across the nation—older blacks admitting that even they are afraid of this new cohort of young, fatherless black males that shoots and kills nihilistically. "You got to be afraid of somebody who just doesn't care," said Johnnie, the organizer. But later, when Barack was alone in his apartment, he realized that he was not afraid. "Wandering through Altgeld and other tough neighborhoods, my fears were always internal: the old fears of not belonging."

The ache at the center of *Dreams from My Father* is this seemingly permanent ache of not belonging. From adolescence onward, Barack Obama pursues the elusive grail of belonging as if his legitimacy as a human being depends on it. It is clearly the ongoing drama that frames his life. And in this quest, unlike with his father, no disappointment in the reality of black life can break his heart.

Does all his effort and sacrifice deliver him to belonging?

Not quite. The post-sixties black American identity is a pitiless taskmaster. And for marginal types like Obama, it makes the price of authenticity higher even than community organizing. To be a "true" black, a "down" brother or sister, a slight corruption is also called for. One must develop a little habit of self-betrayal.

\*     \*     \*

In his organizing work, Obama comes to know a black nationalist who argues with chilling certainty that race is destiny. "It's about blood, Barack, looking after your own. Period." His name is Rafiq, and he stands for a street-hip black nationalism grounded in a blanket hatred of whites and a belief in "race loyalty above all else. . . ." One would expect Barack Obama, of all people, to see straight through this relic of an ideology, and even to be offended by its clearly racist underpinnings. Instead, this enlightened and earnest young man, with an inter-racial background and an Ivy League education, begins to rationalize his way toward a tolerance of this backward and failed creed, even as he sees Rafiq as a gamer.

And what gives these rationalizations a special pathos is that they put Obama at odds with his own mother. He confesses that it is "painful" to entertain a politics that indulges "rage toward whites generally" because it "con-tradicted the morality my mother had taught me" (not to mention his mother herself). What is this morality? It is the civilized idea that character counts vastly more than race, that "distinctions" have to be made "between indi-viduals of goodwill and those who wished me ill. . . ." Barack Obama owes his very existence to the ascen-dance of this morality in American life. And he acknowl-edges this by referring to the "personal stake" he has in it.

Still, in the very next sentence, he says, "And yet perhaps it was a framework that blacks in this country could no longer afford."

But a more relevant question is whether blacks can afford a black nationalism that tries to make a clannish "blackness" into an agent of transformation. What evidence suggests that this nationalism can lift blacks from the blight of the South Side to the level of, say, Barack Obama himself—a superbly educated man with unlimited opportunities in the American mainstream? Isn't it condescending not to use himself as a measure of black possibility? And did he lift himself up by following the strictures of black nationalism, by embracing his race as an agent of change? Or was it precisely his upbringing within the mainstream—and far away from race ideologies—that stood him so well? And why wouldn't a focus on mainstream success, rather than on blackness, be the best treatment for the ills he encounters on the South Side? If black pride is a quite reasonable and even important goal, doesn't black nationalism—with its dislike of whites, its suspicion of the American mainstream, its faith in blackness as a kind of magic, and its focus on self-respect apart from achievement—make genuine pride all but impossible?

And Barack Obama surely knows this, just as I knew it in my East St. Louis days, when I, too, fellow-traveled a little with black nationalism. I knew that late-sixties black nationalism seduced the most vulnerable with kitschy images of "blackness" but never taught anyone how to build a successful life in the modern world. I knew that it was an ideology of avoidance that drew people downward into middling lives of petty scheming and "gaming" whites, like the life Rafiq fashions for himself in Obama's account. I entertained this nationalism in East St. Louis in order to belong, and in order to be polite. And yet my feet walked me to graduate school at night. I plodded forward in the real world because I knew that nationalism took you nowhere. Still, I wore a dashiki, clenched my fist, sported an Afro, traveled to Africa. The need to belong is one of life's more powerful inclinations.

The term for what I did in East St. Louis is *gesture of identification*—the act of going along with something that we may not entirely believe in to show our identification with our group and our militant disregard for mainstream society. It is a way of belonging. When we gesture identification, we hope for transparency with the group—to become so much of the group that we are the group and the group is us. In totalitarian societies, people are coerced into gesturing their identification frequently. If they fail to gesture, they lose transparency with the group and stand out as separate and troublesome individuals who must be repressed. The gulag, literally or figuratively, awaits them.

The post-sixties black identity is essentially a totalitarian identity. It wants to be an activist identity; it wants black protest to be built into each black person's sense of self. So, it demands a solidarity (transparency) very similar to what totalitarian societies demand. It expects many gestures of identification—a liberal politics and a Democratic Party affiliation among them. The obvious problem is that these gestures, which win us solidarity with the group, very often require us to make sacrifices of integrity and principle. Depending on our background, being transparently "black" can come at the expense of what is important to us as human beings.

This is the double bind, the crucible, really, that sets up Barack Obama to become a bound man. On the one hand, he begins life with so many strikes against a transparent black identity that it is almost inevitable that he would long for one. The absent black father, the mixed-race background, the privileged education, the geographical and cultural remoteness of Hawaii from any large black community—all this makes a kind of identity vacuum out of which one can only yearn. But on the other hand, there is the price he will have to pay for a transparent black identity. There will be parts of himself—family values, beliefs, ambitions, loves—that he will not be able to take with him into the black identity he longs for. These things will have to be forsaken lest they make transparency impossible.

Here is Barack rationalizing a racially exclusive black

nationalism that, were it to prevail, would preclude the very existence of people like himself:

> Desperate times called for desperate measures, and for many blacks, times were chronically desperate. If nationalism could create a strong and effective insularity, deliver on its promise of self-respect, then the hurt it might cause well meaning whites, or the inner turmoil it caused people like me, would be of little consequence.

But what "desperate times" is he referring to? And how could "insularity" be "effective"? How is it that "self-respect" can come from the "promise" of an ideology? And doesn't the word "if" make the whole statement hypothetical, and therefore little more than a gesture of identification—a signal of racial loyalty rather than serious analysis?

Surely, Obama is capable of examining nationalism against the life he has actually lived, against the reality of his mother's devotion, against the multiracial setting of his youth, against the abundant goodwill of countless whites throughout his life, and against the absence of any form of racial nationalism in his early education. In such an examination he would no doubt find principles that might easily generalize to the benefit of inner-city blacks. For example, during the years he attended inferior Indonesian schools, it was his mother who woke him at

4:30 every morning to work with her on a more rigorous American curriculum so that he would not fall behind American students. Was it, then, nationalism or momma that developed the academic skills upon which Obama's successful life was built?

And, on the level of educational policy, wouldn't his own experience suggest that parental commitment be made a top priority in the education of inner-city children? Wouldn't he know that almost nothing overcomes the educational inertia spawned by indifferent or resistant or absent parents? Aren't empty ideas like racial "insularity" or nationalism's "promise of self-respect" simply avoidances of the far more profound problem of parental unreliability? Wouldn't Obama have been more enlightened in his inner-city work by the example of his white mother than by black nationalism?

But, of course, Obama cannot make educational policy out of the self-reliance of his Midwestern mother without breaking his transparency with the current black identity. And this is not simply because his mother is white. It is because self-reliance puts the lie to the underlying premise of today's black identity: that identity is power, that "blackness" is empowering and, thus, an agent for positive change.

But Barack Obama's mother was not empowered by her whiteness when she worked with her son on those early mornings in Indonesia. And, of course, there is no reference to her being motivated by her whiteness. She was simply self-reliant and willing to work for what she wanted as a mother: for her son to have the academic skills necessary for success in life. She was being self-reliant, not white.

The point is that racial identity is not an action. And, most important, it cannot serve as a tool of social uplift. You can be "black" (or white, or Hispanic) without *doing* anything. Self-reliance, on the other hand, is the very psychology of action. To be self-reliant, you must *do*. To embrace the black identity as an agent of social transformation is to embrace an illusion. Think of all the money and effort spent on teaching black children about their heritage as a path to self-esteem. In reality, self-esteem follows effort and accomplishment—*doing* rather than being. The emphasis on the black identity by so many black elites, especially educators, has turned out to be one of the most debilitating forces in black life since the sixties.

All this said, there is still the need to belong. People who belong to the majority race don't self-consciously fret over *racial* identity, because their race does not make them an exception. For them, racial identity is one less thing to worry about. But I grew up black in an America that was still segregated, and my race made me an exception. And so I know myself, to a degree, through this experience of exceptionalism; it is the basis of my racial identity. And my need to *belong* to this identity is profound because racial exceptionalism is a part of who I am as an individual. Possibly, whites can know themselves without much reference to their race. But blacks always have the experience of exceptionalism to contend with, so a rather self-conscious black identity is inevitable.

Actually, I have always liked my little burden of racial exceptionalism. I would not know myself without it. And when someone tells me that I am not really black, I hear their words as a kind of nullification, as a little attempted murder, if only in the figurative sense. I need to belong to what I am. And I can only imagine that Barack Obama feels similarly.

The problem is that today's politicized black identity exacts too high a price for belonging. It wants too much disregard of what is universal and human in us. Thus, the absurd pinch: I cannot be fully myself without belonging, and I cannot belong unless I give up being fully myself.

# CHAPTER SIX

# Two Women

Conventional wisdom holds that biracial people suffer from a kind of twoness. The idea is that each race disqualifies them for the other so that they end up with no home in either race. This is a stereotype made for melodrama, and some of the first commercially successful black writing was based on the "tragic mulatto." An example is the beautiful young woman who passes for white and marries the scion of a wealthy white family, only to have a dark-skinned relative turn up and give her away. Then, of course, tragedy and banishment. She is left to live a loveless life in some no-man's-land between the two racial worlds. Out of this ignominy, she becomes either a chaste schoolmarm or a woman available to many men.

Tragic mulatto stories would not work today because

no part of society is really closed to mixed-race people. Today, if Barack Obama feels compelled to belong to the black identity, he is also hounded by the fact that he doesn't have to. He has the option of simply fashioning a life for himself in the broad American mainstream. If he became a broker in Manhattan, say, with a house in Connecticut and a wife who was Brazilian or Japanese or black or white, no one would care. Nothing would happen, except that he might become very rich and, thus, a favorite at charity galas. So, today, there is no tragedy or melodrama in his twoness.

Obama's racial quest springs from a personal angst, not from an oppression in society. In fact, his great nemesis in his pursuit of transparent blackness is not white racism but the lack of it—the temptations of this new open and seductive America that so easily absorbs people like him. The arc of Barack Obama's life is something of a zigzag between his passion to be black and the siren call of extraordinary, even glamorous, opportunities in the American mainstream where the racial identity he longs for matters little. He moves from being a college militant to a researching job at a New York consulting house to community organizing work in Chicago to Harvard Law School and then back to Chicago to practice civil rights law. Blackness does not tempt him away from the mainstream; rather, the mainstream tempts him away from blackness. Two women in his early life embody these mainstream temptations.

\*    \*    \*

Joyce is a young woman Obama encounters in college just as he is launching an all-out—and amazingly self-conscious—crusade to realize his black identity. He says:

> To avoid being mistaken for a sellout, I chose my friends carefully. The more politically active black students. The foreign students. The Chicanos. The Marxist professors and structural feminists and punk rock performance poets. . . . [We] discussed neocolonialism, Franz Fanon, Eurocentrism, and patriarchy.

This is the Obama Joyce meets one day on campus, a young man who has embraced black alienation as a kind of happiness. Like Obama, Joyce is from a mixed-race background and she is apparently quite beautiful— "green eyes and honey skin and pouty lips." Obama seems to be halfheartedly hitting on her when he asks her if she is going to a Black Student Association meeting across campus. But the question only puts up a wall between them. She looks at him "funny" and then, in words that must have stunned Obama, says, "I am not black. I'm *multiracial.*" She tells him that her father is Italian—"the sweetest man in the world"—and that her mother is African, French, and Native American. "Why should I have to choose between them?" she asks. Then she makes a speech:

> It's not white people who are making me choose. Maybe it used to be that way, but now they're willing to treat me like a person. No—it's *black people* who always have to make everything racial. *They're* the ones making me choose. *They're* the ones who are telling me I can't be who I am.

Joyce opposes blackness out of the same determination to claim an identity that drives Obama to embrace blackness. Essentially, she does not accept the "one drop" rule—one drop of black blood making a person black. This rule was conceived in slavery to keep the white race "pure" by making sure that mixed-race slaves (from the dalliances of slave owners with slave women) could not "become" white. (Thomas Jefferson's slave mistress, Sally Hemings, was only one-quarter black, and her children only one-eighth, yet all were kept as slaves.) If this rule is absurd on its face, Joyce's rejection of it—even today— stands as radical. We still live by slavery's insistence that people be either black or white—that race and color correspond to slavery's great dichotomy between free men and slaves. Joyce feels oppressed by this anachronism, and she is determined to build her identity in opposition to it.

But Obama is bent on establishing his black "creden-

tials," and he condescends to "poor Joyce." He is determined to distance himself both from her and from his
own mainstream American past. Above all, he wants
*not* to associate with blacks like himself—blacks from
integrated backgrounds and good preparatory schools
who are at ease in the American mainstream. Yet, in the
long run, these self-imposed restrictions are unsustain-
able. The fact is that Joyce represents a remarkable new
option in American life, one that will always seduce
Obama when the sacrifices of "being black" become
too much. This new option derives from something
Joyce said: white Americans are "willing to treat me like
a person." They no longer impose the absurd "one drop"
rule and no longer force people "to choose." Racialism,
she says, is now the province of blacks who—like the old
slave owners—press people to definitively "choose."
Blacks are "the ones who are telling me I can't be who
I am."

Joyce is saying something to Obama that no one like
her could have said before the civil rights victories of the
sixties: that she trusts mainstream America with her
mixed-race background more than she trusts black
America. Whites treat her "like a person"; blacks "make
everything racial." Joyce is Obama's troublesome doppel-
gänger. As he grinds through the little self-betrayals that
help him belong to blackness and gestures his identification in every way he can, she is that ghostly whisper saying that he is going in the wrong direction. What you

want, she murmurs—the chance to be yourself, racial self-acceptance—is not with blackness; it is in the same American mainstream you came from.

But Joyce, for all her mixed-race insight, is only voicing a theme that has always been present in black life, just as it is present in all minority cultures: the theme of leaving. Toward the end of his community organizing days on the South Side, Obama starts to feel considerable survivor's guilt about leaving these decimated black neighborhoods for arguably the best law school in the country—and, thus, for a new mainstream life of unimaginable possibilities. He expects to encounter resentment from the people he will leave behind, and he feels the need to explain himself. But Johnnie, his fellow organizer, needs no explanation. "I *knew* it," he says when Obama first mentions his plans. Asked how he knew, Johnnie says, "Damn, Barack . . . 'cause you got *options,* that's why. 'Cause you *can* leave. . . . [W]hen somebody's got a choice between Harvard and Roseland, it's only so long somebody's gonna keep choosing Roseland."

So Johnnie knows what Joyce knows. Those who can leave do leave, and are usually better off for it. Assimilation, not blackness, is the road to success. But for Obama—to the mainstream born and without the security of knowing himself within the group—yet more emphasis on assimilation might well feel like laboring to become nobody. After all, he was in Chicago to get to know himself within the group, within its cultural specificity and its character. Sure, success required leaving, but Obama had also left the mainstream to find himself on the black South Side. Leaving the South Side, even for the best of reasons, was to risk losing the black self he had worked so hard to erect.

Perhaps this was the anxiety—this fear of losing the idea of himself as black—that finally came between Obama and the white girl he had fallen in love with after college in New York. For almost a year, they had lived inside their "own private world" with a shared language and customs. Even her family, when they went for a weekend to her family's country house, was nothing less than gracious. But while he was there, standing in her grandfather's impressive study, he had an epiphany. She was from a very different world than his. "And I knew that if we stayed together I'd eventually live in hers. After all, I'd been doing it most of my life. Between the two of us, I was the one who knew how to live as an outsider."

Obama knows all too well what the future will be like with this woman. If their relationship became enduring—and surely they would want it to if they married— he would be permanently consigned to a life in the American mainstream. In other words, he would be back where he had started, back with that old racial anomie and identity ambiguity that had been the suffering of his youth. After all, it was life in the mainstream that had given him the hunger to know himself as black. And maybe, as much as anything else, he was tired of feeling that hunger, tired of having it control the arc of his life. Maybe he wanted to resolve it once and for all. So then he looked into the future with this woman and saw his past. He had begun to build a black self—to take on a racial specificity—and whatever snares and delusions this direction might hold in store, he would at least be covering new ground.

And so, he began to push her away. They fought one night outside a theater after seeing an "angry" black play. She couldn't understand why "black people were so angry all the time." In the car afterward she cried, saying she would be black if she could, but she couldn't. She could "only be herself, and wasn't that enough." Obama's sister, Auma, who hears him recount this story, says finally and accurately, "That's a sad story, Barack." He confesses that when he thinks of what she said that night, "it somehow makes me ashamed."

Little wonder. He rejected her because of her race. And this surely required what race-based decisions have always required—that we serve race at the expense of what is human in us (thus his feeling of shame). Here was a gesture of identification that required a measure of cold-heartedness. And yet, was his decision strength or weakness?

I used to laugh when my own mother—married to my father until death them did part—would say, "You know, interracial marriage is not for everyone." She was never impressed to meet another interracial couple, never patted them on the back for being courageous. People had to truly know themselves, she believed. They had to accept both the freedom to live as they chose and the price they would pay for doing so. What seems clear is that Barack Obama is a man who truly wants to be black, a man who is determined to *resolve* the ambiguity he was born into.

Does this disqualify Obama for the presidency? It may. There is a price to be paid even for fellow-traveling with a racial identity as politicized and demanding as today's black identity. This identity wants to take over a greater proportion of the self than other racial identities do. It wants to have its collective truth—its defining ideas of grievance and protest—become *personal* truth. And then it wants to make loyalty to this truth a reflex within the self, within one's own thoughts, so that all competing thoughts are conceived in disloyalty. A perfectly internalized censorship. To be "authentically black" is to think more *as a black* than as one's self.

And the terms of this identity are very clear. You must join a politics that keeps alive the idea of white obligation to blacks. Social determinism must be your worldview, so that you can see blacks as "systemically" and "structurally" aggrieved even when no actual oppression is apparent. You may mention black responsibility in relation to black uplift, but to "be black," you must always land on a deterministic explanation of black difficulty. Determinism automatically blames and obligates white power for black problems, so it becomes the central faith of the black identity. When a black argues against it, he invokes the Uncle Tom label. Such is the enmeshment of politics, ideas, and history in today's black identity.

The point is not that Barack Obama is a blind and true-believing follower of this identity. Few blacks are. The point is that he is accountable to it. If, for example, Obama broke with this determinism by saying that blacks themselves were largely responsible for closing the academic achievement gap with whites, he would likely be seen as an Uncle Tom for letting whites "off the hook." So, in order to *be black,* he must pay tribute to a determinism that makes whites ultimately responsible for black uplift, even when it is obvious that only black responsibility will make a difference.

These are the identity pressures within which Barack Obama lives. He is vulnerable to them because he has hungered for a transparent black identity much of his life. He needs to "be black." And this hunger—no matter how understandable it may be—means that he is not in a position to reject the political liberalism inherent in his racial identity. For Obama, liberalism *is* blackness.

So, too much of the Obama who grew up in Hawaii

and Indonesia is lost to the Obama who joins a South Side black church with a "Black Value System," focused on "Black freedom," the "black community," and the "black family." In this church, the adjective "black" is a more consistent theme than any of the nouns it modifies. It is invoked as an atavism, a God-given specialness that is thought meaningful in itself. It is a claim not just of racial difference but of racial difference to the point of an essential superiority. "Blackness" is always an assertion of racial superiority. Add it to the human universals like "community" and "family" and "freedom" and you get the illusion of a black Golden Age, a time when a deep and true blackness defined all these things. But Golden Age illusions tend to console more than inspire.

Few black people are better situated to know this than Barack Obama. That he would join a church this steeped in blackness, with so many other churches available, only underscores his determination to be transparently black. How else to reconcile this church membership (and for over a decade) with the fact of his own family—his white mother, grandmother, and grandfather. It was not a "Black Value System" that prepared Obama so well for the world. Nor was it "black community" or "black family." It was not black anything. One could easier argue that his good luck was to be born into a white "family," "community," and "value system." And, in fact, isn't his success, his ease in the American mainstream, due more to assimilation than to blackness? Isn't his great advantage over other blacks precisely his exposure from infancy on to mainstream culture? And doesn't it then follow that *assimilation* might be a very reasonable strategy for black uplift? And, correspondingly, doesn't Obama's success make the precise point that "blackness" is a dead end?

So how can Barack Obama sit every week in a church preaching blackness and not object—not stand and proclaim that he was raised quite well, thank you, by three white Middle Westerners? More important, how can he not let his actual experience inform his ideas and his politics? Who would be better positioned to know that values have nothing to do with race, or that assimilation is really about mastery and development rather than self-hate and cultural infidelity? And who better to know that the adjective "black" imparts no special knowledge when attached to words like "family" and "freedom?" Isn't America's fascination with him precisely his potential for defusing race as a national obsession? Might this not be his Promethean fire, his special gift to his times?

But Obama is also the kind of man who can close down the best part of himself to *belong* to this black church and, more broadly, to the black identity. This is the sort of habit that, over time, can leave a person without much of a self. What are the insights that come out of his full human experience, and where is the faith that his own truth must count? I worry when he says (as he so often does), "I'm not an ideologue." The other side of this campaign mantra may be that he has no deep convictions, that he may have actually avoided thinking things through to their first principles so as to be more malleable, more things to more people.

Obama seems most pained when he is pressed for his true beliefs. The habit of not going with oneself—of not making one's politics accountable to one's actual experience—can make a person more protean than Promethean. Woody Allen's Zelig character comes to mind, a man who can fit imperceptively into every background, who can hunt with the dogs and run with the foxes. I don't believe that Obama is a Zelig, but most of his policy recommendations have this dogs-and-foxes quality. He will say, for example, that a little affirmative action is good for blacks, but maybe it's also good for poor whites. Yet he is loath to say how racial preferences stack up with his principles, his concept of democracy. Thus far, Obama is the very opposite of a Reaganlike conviction politician.

Strong convictions seem to be anathema to Barack Obama because he is a bound man. He has fit himself into the world by often taking his own experience *out* of account. If he takes his actual experience into account, he will lose the black identity—the cultural specificity, the sense of groundedness and belonging—that he has worked so hard to secure. So he simply cannot acknowledge the full truth of his own experience. He is bound against himself.

But he is also bound by forces outside himself, forces of history and culture and politics that bind and squeeze him even more tightly than his internal pressures. His presidential bid is indeed something new, but the landscape he traverses is very old.

PART II

# The Society

# CHAPTER SEVEN

# Masking

I possess a photographic portrait of Louis Armstrong that I treasure greatly. It must have been taken on a hot summer evening fairly late in his life. In it, he is wearing a short-sleeved shirt completely unbuttoned in front; interestingly, a Star of David hangs from his neck on a thin chain that glints in the sunlight. His right arm rests on its elbow so that his powerful right hand is conspicuously next to his face, almost like a second face. Pinched between thumb and forefinger of this hand—in the characteristic dope smoker's grip—is a half-smoked joint that sends a faint trellis of smoke up into the summer air. I was stunned the first instant I laid eyes on this photograph, but not for its novelty of capturing a celebrity in the act of smoking a joint. It was the look on Armstrong's face that grabbed me. It is perfectly frank and guileless. The eyes are sad, willful, and faintly angry all at the same time. Most of all, they seem tired and quite beyond amusement, as if they have seen absolutely everything there is to see.

I love the photograph because its image is a million miles away from the iconic image of Louis Armstrong—the tritely happy figure on the bandstand with the trademark white handkerchief, the broken lip, and the self-effacing grin. This is the real man behind that mask in his full depth and complexity, looking exactly like who he really was: one of the twentieth century's greatest artists. So nice—even soothing—to see Louis Armstrong as he really was.

I also cherish this photograph as a kind of cultural artifact because, in its sharp contrast with the familiar image of Armstrong, it symbolizes masking, one of the most interesting and troublesome cultural characteristics of black American life. Masking is as simple as the fashioning of a face for the world—"a face to meet the faces that we meet," as T. S. Eliot once put it. As the word itself makes clear, the mask is not an authentic representation of one's true self; rather, it is a presentation of oneself that angles for advantage.

Imagine Louis Armstrong, born poor, black, and fatherless, growing up in New Orleans at the beginning of the twentieth century, the era in which Jim Crow was entrenching itself across the entire South. White supremacy was being openly written into the law. A system of racial apartheid was being erected and then enforced by the terrorism of lynchings, house burnings, beatings, etc. This was the world in which Armstrong discovered his musical genius. And conversely, it was his genius that propelled him into this larger world and forced him to negotiate it. He was too good to linger his life away on the black side of apartheid. Talent gave him a life on the white side, too. How to handle it?

Louis Armstrong adapted a mask that came out of the black minstrel tradition. It was certainly not as sycophantic and self-demeaning as the blackface caricatures of the actual minstrel shows. Still, it did the one thing it had to do. It communicated to white audiences that Louis Armstrong would entertain them but not presume to be their equal. The relentlessly beaming smile, the handkerchief dabbing away the sweat, the reflexive bowing, the exaggerated humility and graciousness—all this signaled that he would not breach the manners of segregation, the propriety that required him to be both cheerful and less than fully human.

In other words, Armstrong's mask was a small offering of black inferiority. It was something he had to give to whites—at least a slight concurrence with their mythology of white supremacy and black inferiority. This also amounted to a gift of innocence to whites, because it said that their racism was not prejudice but truth—a truth he himself observed. And this little gift of innocence—this slight homage to whiteness—was a part of the show; it helped white people in a segregated society enjoy themselves without guilt. And it enabled them to cherish Louis Armstrong.

For the oppressed—and even for those who simply belong to minority groups—masking is always an attempt to offset the power differential that so favors those born to the mainstream. Armstrong's mask allowed him to exercise power in a society bent on keeping power away from his kind. It helped him offset the power differential with whites by giving him a livelihood in the broad American mainstream that he was not meant to have. Bing Crosby, to the mainstream born, did not have to wear a mask of racial self-effacement in order to win an audience. The masks that blacks wear in American society are always *strategic,* always based on a *reading* of what is possible in white America.

And so, we blacks are never quite what whites think we are. Our entire history in America is a history of, among other things, masking. Today's ferocious black obsession with unity—particularly among the black leadership—is simply an obsession with giving the group mask the uniformity it needs to be powerful. Our manipulation of whites requires that we all be on the same page, behind the same mask. Whites have trouble reading blacks because we are always showing them only what we want them to see, always pushing them this way and that. We always have two narratives: what we tell each other and what we tell whites.

\*       \*       \*

Miles Davis, the twentieth century's greatest jazz trum-
peter after Armstrong, often turned his back to his audiences. His surliness was so legendary that fans considered
it a badge of honor to have been abused by him. Today
I know an elderly white gentleman who likes to glamour
himself by telling the story—almost every time I see
him—of being cursed out by Miles Davis at Shelley's
Manhole in Los Angeles back in the sixties. I, too, saw
Miles play on a few occasions and was once, also to my
great honor, cursed out by him. His mask was that he
had no mask. And one of my pleasures at his shows,
along with his music, was simply looking at him. His
face was so without affect that it could be described as
existential. My joke was that Sartre could have pho-
tographed him and been done with it.

And yet, it was a mask—maybe not so far removed
from the actual man as Armstrong's mask, but a mask
nevertheless. Miles emerged in a more prosperous postwar America that was building toward the civil rights victories of the sixties. President Truman had integrated the
military; the Supreme Court had moved to integrate the
schools. And jazz had evolved—to the displeasure of
many—from a music to dance by into a modernist art
form of deep individual expression. Miles's eminently
cool mask communicated two things: that he was an
artist rather than an entertainer and that he was utterly

unapologetic as a black. These, then, were the terms of his engagement with the broad American mainstream.

In Armstrong's day, Miles could not have turned his back on white audiences or cursed people between sets and survived. He would have had no career. Yet his mask worked in postwar America, and it worked in the same way that Armstrong's mask had worked decades earlier. Miles, too, offered his white audiences the chance for a little innocence. The America of his era—particularly the urban North—was ready for racial change, and there was no better way to show one's racial broad-mindedness and artistic hipness than by going to see a black jazz artist who insulted you a little. If Armstrong helped whites to innocence by going along a bit with white supremacy, Miles did it by giving whites a chance to see superiority in him—this menacing and subversive black hipster who took white women for granted and drove around Manhattan in a Ferrari. For whites, there was self-flattery in being the fan of either man.

Different eras, different masks. And it was Armstrong's fate to live well into the Miles Davis era so that his mask fell out of phase with the times and turned on him. In my youth, in the fifties and sixties, Louis Armstrong was quite unfairly seen by many as an Uncle Tom, while Miles Davis was thought to embody a new uncompromising militance. In my black neighborhood, we gave Armstrong no credit for having emerged in an era when white supremacy was a totalitarian blanket over black life. We wanted to have the illusion that blacks had never been forced to display his kind of humility. In our protest era he shamed us, and we often held him up to ridicule. No doubt he suffered greatly from this in his last years. Actually, Armstrong kicked up quite a controversy in the fifties by criticizing the segregationist Arkansas governor, Orval Faubus, in rougher language than any civil rights leader of that day would have used. He was the first black entertainer to demand—by contract—that he be able to stay at the same hotels he performed in. At some risk to his own career, Armstrong "opened" some of America's largest hotels to blacks. He was no Uncle Tom. Our mistake, if not our shame, was to confuse the mask with the man.

But the maskings of Louis Armstrong and Miles Davis are only personal examples of the masking that we black Americans also do on a collective level. That is, we also have a distinct group mask that we are all expected to wear, if only loosely. And this group mask, like the individual mask, is always *strategic,* always based on a *reading* of what is possible for us in broader white America. Our history in America is a history of having to negotiate our fate *indirectly* through white America. So, to affect our fate we have always had to manipulate white America, to find the collective face that would best win us advantage with whites.

The great debates in black American history have essentially been over strategy and mask. The black Talented Tenth of the late nineteenth century—the first significant black middle class—believed that identifying with white America, subscribing to the norms of middle-class life, identifying with the American Dream, practicing piety, and carrying a little contempt for the unwashed black masses would be the best strategy for getting ahead. To this end, they presented themselves essentially as colored versions of middle-class whites. Their reading was that whites would see how alike they were and be shamed into granting them full equality. It was a terrible misreading, since white America was retrenching along racial lines, not opening up. So, here was a mask that did not work very well.

It was Booker T. Washington who had a more accurate reading of whites. He saw that whites simply would not tolerate racial equality or even much protest toward that end. So he advocated development rather than equality, and he favored a mask that showed blacks as humble, hard working, and accommodating of segregation. Washington's great nemesis, W. E. B. Dubois, wanted the opposite—a mask of protest. Later, in the great civil rights era, we wanted to be the face of universal humanity. We wanted our race to be incidental. If whites could see our humanity, they would be morally compelled to offer us full equality. This argument and mask worked so well that it led to a new era of white guilt in which whites—particularly institutions—had to redeem their moral authority through blacks. And so today, continuing to read white America as we always have, we wear a mask focused on our racial difference rather than our common humanity. White American institutions do not want our humanity per se; they want our race today because it helps them build the "diversity" that fends off the perception that they are racist.

Therefore, to live as a black American means that you belong to a group that continually reinvents itself *in relation* to a dominant group. It means that we blacks tend to know ourselves—collectively—through our strategic relations to whites. One of the most profound problems in black American life is that our strategic masks—the faces we put on to seek advantage through white America—invariably become our racial identity. In other words, we come to think of ourselves *as* our mask. Certainly there is an enduring black American culture apart from masking but, within a given era, the collective mask(s) too often define our identity.

A few years back, a white journalist told me that he had recently interviewed a well-to-do black doctor on the subject of racial profiling. This doctor drove a Mercedes, lived in an upscale, largely white suburb of a large Midwestern city, and was rightly proud of how far he had come from his inner-city beginnings. The doctor told the journalist that he had been stopped by the police while driving in his own neighborhood "at least twenty times" simply because he was a black in an expensive car in a largely white neighborhood. The white journalist asked me what I thought about this, and I said that I believed the doctor was lying. The journalist was aghast. The doctor, he said, had seemed perfectly sincere.

I am sure that he was sincere. I am also sure that he was lying. It is not plausible that this perfectly dignified black doctor was stopped *twenty* times in his own neighborhood simply for being a black and in an expensive car. Maybe one time, or two times, or maybe not at all, but twenty times defies reason. Surely in today's environment, and in an upscale suburb, more than one such stop of the same wealthy black man would bring the local police department under threat of a lawsuit. And wouldn't the local papers love the story of the good Dr. So-and-So being stopped twenty times solely because of his race? I can imagine a huge financial settlement and mandatory diversity training for the entire police department.

So, yes, the doctor was not being truthful, and yet he was being consistent with his idea of himself. Today, racial victimization is the face we blacks want broader America to see because it entitles blacks and obligates whites. This is our strategic mask, and so we make it our identity. We say of ourselves that, no matter how high we climb or how much we play by the rules, we can still be victimized and harassed because of our race. This is *who* we are, and it is delusional for us to think otherwise. So when the good doctor says "twenty times," he is speaking the poetic truth of his black identity. It may register with him very slightly that "twenty times" is an exaggeration, but he is comfortable in the feeling that he is speaking a more accurate truth than the facts would allow.


Does Barack Obama wear a mask?

To "be black" in America—to self-consciously pursue a black identity as Obama does—one must join a strategy toward America, a politics that tries to manipulate the American mainstream. This requires a mask—a face that will help the group in its manipulation. And this mask must be built around the group's best case for itself. A truly good mask will try to make the poetic truth—the doctor's "twenty times"—pass for the literal truth. It will show white America a "twenty times" black world and demand redress accordingly.

When Obama joins Trinity United Church of Christ on the South Side, with its monochrome focus on blackness, the main theme of the black mask is spelled out for him: he must think and act in the world as if the exaggerated poetic truth of white racism is the literal truth. His minister lectures him that only race—and not social class—matters for blacks. "Cops don't check my bank account when they pull me over and make me spread-eagle against the car," he tells Barack. "Life's not safe for a black man in this country, Barack. Never has been. Probably never will be." Especially offensive to the minister is William Julius Wilson's well-known book, *The Declining Significance of Race.* "Now what country is he living in?" he asks. Racism is this minister's great strategic advantage; it gives him an almost demagogic power and a racial moral authority that distinguishes his church from its competitors. He offers his parishioners as much racial redemption as religious redemption. And if race is now of "declining significance," then so is he. So, effectively, he defines the black identity as a faith in the pervasiveness of white racism. He is blackest who believes most strongly in white racism. This is his implicit lesson for Obama.

Barack's wife, Michelle, wore this mask well in their *60 Minutes* interview: "Barack is black. He can be shot on the way to the gas station." Here, fitting her mask snuggly over her face, she offers poetic truth as literal truth. Before the popularity of Obama's presidential candidacy (he is now justifiably under Secret Service protection), he was at virtually no risk of being shot by a white racist on the way to the gas station. However, he might well have been at risk of violence from a young black gangbanger. But the "blackness" mask does not allow for such distinctions, or wants them blurred. It does not matter that reality in no way supports Michelle's point. She is telling the larger truth of black victimization in America. She is facilitating her race's manipulation of the American mainstream. Her mask is perfectly in place.

The problem here for Barack, of course, is that his racial identity commits him to a manipulation of the very society that he seeks to lead. To "be black," he has to exaggerate black victimization in America. And he has to argue for public policy that responds to the exaggeration rather than to the reality of victimization. Worse, his identity will pressure him to see black difficulties— achievement gaps, high illegitimacy rates, high crime rates, family collapse, and so on—in the old framework of racial oppression. The black identity still wants to see racism as the great demon in black life. It never wants to see blame cast on blacks themselves. And it believes that, even when blacks are clearly the source of their own problems, government will always be the great agent of social transformation, if only it will be generous and compassionate.

None of this is to say that Obama would simply be a sap for his black identity. He is, in fact, quite good at articulating black responsibility (his Selma speech at the anniversary of the march across Edmund Pettus Bridge that triggered the 1965 Voting Rights Bill). Perhaps the problem is that his long struggle with identity— his struggle to fit himself into the black mask—has tempered his imagination itself so that he sees blacks, finally, as society's children. At the very least, he may feel predisposed to wear the mask for them, to keep alive the idea of masking itself as a black American strategy for advancement.

71

His great opportunity, of course, is to point the way beyond masking, manipulation, and poetic truth. This possibility is a large part of his attractiveness in the mainstream. But here, again, is his problem of bounded-ness—to go toward the mainstream injures him with blacks, and vice versa. Making all this worse is the fact that there are *two* great masks available to blacks—two ways that blacks can appear and two ways that whites can see them. These are old ways of seeing in America. They are automatic and well beneath the level of conscious thought. And they bestow on Barack Obama what Ralph Ellison has called a very "complex fate."

# CHAPTER EIGHT

# Bargaining and Challenging

Bargaining and challenging are the two great masks that we blacks wear when we seek success and power in the American mainstream. They are identities of a sort. They come replete with belief systems and a politics, even a psychology. People seem naturally inclined toward one or the other, but bargainers can sometimes challenge and challengers can sometimes bargain. The very fact that *racial* masking is still an aspect of black life makes the point that many of us—consciously or unconsciously—still feel we must navigate the predispositions of the white majority in order to win success and power. This is the existential circumstance that makes bargaining and challenging timeless features of black American culture.

Both these masks enable blacks to set up an exchange

with white America in which innocence is traded for power. These masks were always features of black culture. No doubt, slaves bargained with and challenged their masters. But since the sixties, both masks have become far more common for two reasons: more blacks have sought success and power in the mainstream and whites have endured a collapse of moral authority in racial matters. The sixties stigmatized white Americans with the racial sins of the past—with the bigotry and hypocrisy that countenanced slavery, segregation, and white supremacy. Now, to win back moral authority, whites— and especially American institutions—must prove the negative: that they are not racist. In other words, white America has become a keen market for racial innocence, and this is the new underlying condition that elicits so much bargaining and challenging.

Blacks, on the other hand—now fully acknowledged as America's long-suffering victims—possess a largesse of moral authority that whites simply can never have. And this amounts to a currency of power in a society that now needs moral authority around race for the very legitimacy of its institutions. Of course, whites cannot bestow racial innocence on themselves. Thus the market in which blacks sell and whites buy.

When bargainers in any walk of life seek success in the American mainstream, they make a very specific deal with whites (individuals and institutions): *I will not use America's horrible history of white racism against you, if you will promise not to use my race against me.* In other words, bargainers grant whites the innocence and moral authority they need in return for their goodwill and generosity. Bargainers give before they ask, and they trust that reciprocity will prevail—that goodwill will elicit goodwill. Bargaining is effective because it begins in magnanimity.

In the eighties, *The Cosby Show* made the classic bargainer's deal with its vast white audience. Bill Cosby said, in effect, look, I'm a comedian, an artist of a kind, and I want to practice my art. I want to share it with the world, and I believe you will appreciate it. Therefore, you can turn on my program every week and be assured that you will not have the ugly legacy of white racism rubbed in your face. Instead, I will judge you by your better instincts and trust that you will rise to that judgment. In fact, you can watch my show and feel that you are transcending that odious little corner of the human soul wherein racism flourishes. You can relate to black characters in a human rather than racial context. So you will get something that even the funniest white sit-coms cannot offer: a sense of racial innocence, a pride in your ability to humanly identify with black people. And in return, I only want the privilege of entertaining you.

It was a good deal. *The Cosby Show* was one of the most successful situation comedies in television history. Cliff Huxtable was America's father. Of course, the show was also a superbly written weekly morality play with engaging characters, and it would surely have succeeded without the element of bargaining. Still, bargaining allowed it to offer something quite rare in sit-com television: the opportunity for whites to have a human identification across racial lines. This was an offering of innocence, and it gave the show a patina of racial idealism and good faith.

But bargaining also works in the everyday affairs of everyday people. In the professions, the corporate world, government agencies—in that large black middle and upper middle class—bargaining is the norm, almost a form of good manners. On the job the ambitious black makes a little gift of innocence to white colleagues by signaling that he or she is not the kind of person who forages for opportunities to cry racism. This is a gift of innocence because it flatters whites with the presumption that they will not be racist in this workplace. It gives whites a way to feel proud of themselves, and a goal to live up to. When bargained with in this way, whites themselves come to have an investment in making sure that the environment is clear of racism. Bargaining has granted them a good reputation to protect. So racism becomes something whites, too, will not tolerate for the damage it does to their own good name. The beauty of bargaining is that it turns the black desire to live without racism into a white self-interest.

Of course, bargaining is still a mask, a strategy, a manipulation. We practice it in the *hope* that whites will live up to the racial innocence we ascribe to them. But we don't know for certain that they will. Bargainers gamble that their own display of good faith will push whites into their better selves.

When challengers reach for success and power in the American mainstream, they never give whites the benefit of the doubt. Quite the opposite, they use their moral authority as blacks to stigmatize whites as born racists. Challengers presume whites to be guilty of racism in the same way that bargainers presume them innocent—as a strategic manipulation. Challengers put all whites in the position of having to chase after their racial innocence. The challenger's code: *whites are incorrigibly racist until they do something to prove otherwise.*

Among blacks, challengers have no special power. But the instant they enter the American mainstream, the moral authority that goes with their black skin garners them enormous power. In a society where the greatest shame has been white racism, they have power over the guilt and innocence of whites. They can apply or remove what is arguably the most powerful stigma in American life: the racist stigma. This is a great power because it gives challengers a degree of control over the moral legitimacy of people and institutions. Nothing in American life ruins a career faster than the racist stigma.

For uttering three clearly racist words ("nappy-

headed hos"), the radio host Don Imus famously under-
went something like career vaporization. A thirty-five-
year career in one of the country's toughest industries
was completely stilled within days of his reckless remark.
Once a person or an institution is stigmatized in this
way, they become radioactive, the worst kind of pariah.
To stand next to them is to be in the shadow of stigma.
Imus's corporate sponsors fled immediately, fearing that
the products they sell to the American people would have
the taint of racism. Even a promotional tour for a new
book by Imus's wife, scheduled to begin on the day he
stepped down, had to be cancelled. Despite days of abject
and moving apology, and even the forgiveness of the
women he had offended on the Rutgers women's basketball team, Imus found himself quite beyond redemption.

Interestingly, the first man that Imus ran to see
while in the depths of his ignominy was the Reverend Al
Sharpton, clearly the most conspicuous challenger at
work in America today. Sharpton is not wealthy, leads no
movement, and is unelected to any office, yet he is a self-
appointed arbiter of the racist stigma and, thus, a powerful man. Like a modern-day potentate, he can ruin or
redeem a white man in one quick trip to the micro-
phones. And though he has himself committed many of
the sins that so outrage him in whites, he pays no price
and loses no power when his hypocrisy is pointed out.
The moral authority of simply being black, in a society
shamed and compromised by its past treatment of blacks,

makes Sharpton immune from the consequences he forces on white sinners. Rather than a pariah, he becomes a kind of priest. And so it was that Don Imus, hungering for redemption, got into a car, traveled uptown, and offered himself up for dispensation on Al Sharpton's radio show.

Why didn't Imus go to visit Colin Powell? After all, Secretary Powell is a highly esteemed and lustrously accomplished American who is also black. How is it that he lacks Al Sharpton's powers of dispensation? Imus knew instinctively that someone like Powell would be no good for his purposes. Colin Powell is not a man who wields the racist stigma as his main source of power in American life. He is far more a bargainer than a challenger, someone who enters the American mainstream in the good faith that he will meet something like fairness. Sharpton, with little education or talent beyond being fast on his feet—with no background for mainstream success—relies entirely on the power of racial stigmatizing to make his way in America. He lives off the moral authority of his race's long suffering in America; Powell lives on his talents and energies as an individual—and his faith, nervous though it may be, that America can be fair to blacks. He has no special racial imprimatur to dispense. I'm sure it never crossed Imus's mind to visit him.

Only a challenger can remove the racist stigma from whites with finality—and then only when they get something in return for the innocence they dispense. Challengers put themselves in charge of white innocence. They set the terms for it; they even specify the "politically correct" language it requires. They tell American institutions that they must practice affirmative action and diversity or have their legitimacy destroyed by stigmatization. And so institutions become obsessed with "diversity," not because it is effective in achieving anything, but because it fends off stigma. It keeps the challengers at bay. If Imus ever returns to the airways, his operation will no doubt be swathed in diversity.

# CHAPTER NINE

# The Iconic Negro

In his memoir, *The Measure of a Man,* Sidney Poitier describes some of the behind-the-scenes intrigues and maneuverings that led up to possibly his most famous movie, *Guess Who's Coming to Dinner.* A movie about a young black doctor coming to dinner at the home of a wealthy white family to ask for their daughter's hand in marriage required considerable subterfuge and the most careful negotiations to get off the ground back in the mid-sixties. After all, the civil rights movement, on its deepest level, had been a war against white supremacy, an idea enforced by the taboo against interracial marriage. I remember that in the civil rights era we used to say, "We don't want to marry your daughter; we just want our rights." It was a way of allaying the very worst fear of many whites, that integration would turn into miscegenation. Then, a few years after winning our rights with the great civil rights legislation of the mid-sixties, comes a film like *Guess Who's Coming to Dinner,* which seems to say, "Now we want your daughter, too."

Quite nervous about so radical a project, Katharine Hepburn and Spencer Tracy felt the need to meet Sidney Poitier and take his measure before finally signing on. Now by this time, Sidney Poitier was one of the biggest stars in Hollywood, had been in more than thirty films, and had won the Best Actor Oscar a few years earlier. His measure had been taken many times and was there on the record for all to see. Why the need for more scrutiny? "If it had been Paul Newman they were going to do a movie with, would they have checked him out so thoroughly?" wrote Poitier.

In other words, here was a provocation that might have tempted Poitier to don the challenger's mask. "Should I have been angry and confrontational?" Black power had just then begun to sweep the country, and it admonished blacks no longer to suffer indignities from whites. Whites needed to be backed up, put in their place—retrained, as it were, on how to live without the props of white supremacy. But Sidney Poitier was not a challenger; both on and off screen he was the quintessential bargainer. So he decided to give Hepburn and Tracy "the benefit of the doubt." "I looked at them as ordinary, decent folks. And in fact they turned out to be that—and a hell of a lot more." Here was the classic bargain, the gift of innocence to whites in the hope that they would live up to it. But to get to this happy ending Poitier had to mask, had to subject himself to a scrutiny that Hepburn and Tracy would likely never subject Paul Newman to, and he had to *pretend* that there was no racial offense involved.

In a series of hit movies in the sixties, Sidney Poitier used bargaining to project a new image of black Americans into the culture. His work was an artistic and cultural accompaniment to the civil rights movement. There was the theoretical language of civil rights with all its legal and moral abstractions, and then there was Sidney Poitier, a highly visible embodiment of that full human dignity that blacks wanted projected in those times of change. We blacks watched him very closely and gave him very little room in which to move. Instinctively, we understood bargaining and knew him to be a bargainer. But before Poitier, when white supremacy had reigned unapologetically, the bargainer's gift of innocence to whites had always involved at least a small offering of black inferiority. Some obsequiousness or self-deprecation had to be on view so whites could feel assured that you were not challenging America's racial hierarchy. So we watched to see if Sidney would slip up and laugh a little too happily or utter a double negative or, God forbid, roll an eye. He never did.

There was more reciprocity in Sidney's bargaining than we had ever seen before. He gave no more than the benefit of the doubt to whites and, in return, they got out of his way. His characters knew their own worth and demanded their due. When the southern sheriff in *In the Heat of the Night* slaps him for being uppity, he instantly slaps him back, and the two men stand glaring into each other's eyes. Here was a black man demanding his reciprocity: I gave you the benefit of the doubt and you *will* give me respect. You *will* return the goodwill. Probably no other scene in Poitier's oeuvre better makes the point that he was bargaining in a different America than Louis Armstrong had bargained in.

But Sidney Poitier's career brought to the fore another important feature of bargaining—the gratitude factor. When whites receive the "benefit of the doubt" from blacks—this gift of racial innocence in a society shamed by its history of racism—they are *flattered*. They are being told that they are different from the white American bigots of legend. Despite the horrid reputation of the white race for being blind to the humanity of all other races, they are being trusted—at considerable risk to blacks—to behave in concert with the principle of racial equality. This is an extraordinary gift of trust to whites, coming as it does in a society where the legacy of past racism means that whites still surpass blacks on most socioeconomic measures. The response to this flattering trust is invariably gratitude.

And this gratitude is transmogrified into a real and powerful affection for the black who inspires it. In the case of Sidney Poitier, it meant that, for at least a season, he became the most popular movie star in America, with bigger box office than Paul Newman and Barbra Streisand. In a time when black challengers—Huey Newton, Stokely Carmichael, H. Rap Brown—were the norm, the gratitude for Sidney's "benefit of the doubt" was immense. After the mid-sixties, in what I have called the age of white guilt—an age in which whites have been at pains to prove themselves innocent of racism—there has been a spillover of gratitude for blacks who bargain, blacks who offer innocence and trust.

This is not to say that challengers don't do well in these times as well. There is a desperation in white guilt that feeds both bargainers and challengers. Jesse Jackson and Al Sharpton get no gratitude, but they do get power and considerable money. Still, challengers will never have wide mainstream acceptance in America. They will never have the affection or the love of broader America. Like bargainers, they offer innocence, but only after a kind of extortion that sullies both parties. Bargainers give in good faith and receive in goodwill. And for the very best of them, there is a kind of synergy—a back-and-forth compounding of goodwill—that broadens and deepens the affection and love they receive almost to the point of reverence.

The great bargainer of our time is Oprah Winfrey, arguably the most well-loved public figure in American life. Possibly, it is the extraordinary scope of her gift of innocence that makes her special. Not only does she "give the benefit of the doubt," she puts many of her most daunting personal struggles in the hands of her public. She confesses, she self-examines, she struggles, and she takes responsibility—all on national television most afternoons. Such openness clearly requires courage, but the form her courage takes is the unparalleled level of trust that she puts in her largely white public. She trusts them with far more of her inner life—even her woundedness—than other public personalities. And this trust is her gift of innocence to her white public; it says you are such good human beings that I can trust you with the difficult details of my life. Her audience is rightly flattered, and it sends back waves of gratitude in the form of love, admiration, and affection.

There is a point for black bargainers—Sidney and Oprah are good examples—when the synergy of innocence given and gratitude received elevates them to an iconic status in the culture. What I will call the "iconic Negro" is someone who embodies the highest and best longings of both races. In such people, both blacks and whites can see the historic shames of their races at last overcome. In loving Oprah or in admiring Sidney, whites can experience themselves shorn of racism—as people capable of complete human identification with a black. As white women wrestle with a weight problem or the memory of childhood sexual abuse along with Oprah, they may look up at some point and remember that she is black, but then only laugh at how little that means. And here, in this little laugh of recognition, they see that race in no way separates them from Oprah. They see that the evil of racism is not operative within them, and they admire themselves a little for this. They are quite proud to like Oprah. Iconic Negroes are opportunities for whites to know themselves as people who have simply transcended white racism. For blacks, they represent transcendence of the inferiority stereotype. Oprah is a black woman from a difficult background who has achieved enormous success through her intelligence, charm, business acumen, and perseverance. She has competed against whites and done extremely well on her own merit, thus rendering absurd the charge of black inferiority.

Iconic Negroes arise only in racially divided societies. Certainly Nelson Mandela was such a figure in South Africa. Whites could defend against the shame of their long use of racism as power by finding it in themselves to admire him. Blacks could be consoled in their underdevelopment by taking pride in his greatness. Iconic Negroes are absolution for whites and redemption for blacks. Everyone has an investment in them; everyone takes a protective attitude toward them. They seem to resolve the very divide they straddle.

Because racial divisions seem somehow healed in the person of iconic Negroes, and because they flatter both blacks and whites, they are some of the most compelling personalities in American advertising. Aside from the extraordinary talents that make them famous, there is also the bargainer's racial goodwill, the trust and flattery across racial lines that comes back in gratitude. The Oprah imprimatur on a book will garner far more sales than the imprimatur of even the grandest literary prize. This is because Oprah already has an established reciprocity with her public. She has already flattered them by giving them "the benefit of the doubt," by trusting them not to use her race against her, and by trusting them with many of her most daunting personal struggles. And they have already reciprocated with gratitude and affection. All this is in place when she puts the Oprah sticker on a book. And this sticker is the promise of that same reciprocity. Stories of overcoming inner demons, surviving abuse or racism, conquering physical disabilities, or resurrecting an empty life by finding the answers within one's self—her books do what she does. They flatter readers by *trusting* them to find their better and more compassionate selves. You may not know what you are getting when the words "Pulitzer Prize Winner" are emblazoned on the cover of a book, but when Oprah's sticker is in place you have a clear idea.

Bill Cosby sold vast amounts of Jell-O in the eighties. Coming off his long-running television sit-com, he brought the good feeling of an already established mutuality of trust and gratitude between himself and the public to whatever product he endorsed. Today, Tiger Woods and Michael Jordan are so sublimely talented that their endorsements would be golden no matter what their race. Still, as black bargainers, they bring an additional level of reciprocity with the public to the products they back. Even the despicably infamous O. J. Simpson, in his iconic Negro days, ran through airports for Hertz Rent-a-Car as a black whom everyone was flattered to like.

The iconic Negro is someone who dispels the sense of "otherness" between the races and replaces it with a feeling of warmth, human familiarity, and racial goodwill. In him or her we have the sense that good race relations are really very easy and natural, and that tension between the races is essentially superfluous. When we look at Oprah, it seems so clear that people can "get along" if they simply will. Isn't it just our troublesome racial memories that keep imposing "otherness" on us? Iconic Negroes are people who seem unwilling to be barred from happiness or open relations with people of all groups by their racial memories. Dr. Cliff Huxtable's (Bill Cosby's) racial memory comes out in his avid appreciation of good jazz, not in tense and guarded relations with whites. With whites he is easy and natural. And this is the great contribution of iconic Negroes: they combat racial otherness by showing it to be silly and tiresome and small.

Nevertheless, this contribution is utterly contingent

on their wearing the bargainer's mask. In fact, one of the most important qualities iconic Negroes must have is the discipline it takes to wear this mask. Their problem is that their full unmasked selves always jeopardize their iconic persona. They are most at risk from themselves. And they are always in the position of having to discipline themselves into the contours of the mask—of having to suppress certain racial feelings that might contradict the mask. Even if the mask is as open to self-exploration as Oprah's, there will be some suppression of genuine racial feelings and ideas.

Sidney Poitier felt that Hepburn and Tracy were a bit racially insensitive when they so thoroughly scrutinized him at such an advanced point in his career. If Sidney lacked discipline, if he let them somehow see his pique at such treatment, he would lose the capacity to offer them the "benefit of the doubt." Instead of offering them innocence, he would offer them suspicion. He would make them wonder if their lack of experience with blacks, with "others" of any kind, didn't make them, at the very least, inadvertently racist. They would feel accused and under pressure to show themselves as good people—people free of racism. How would their inevitable resentment work as all three collaborated on a movie that protests the smallmindedness of racism?

So Sidney, like all bargainers, disciplined himself and stayed within the contours of his mask. And, of course, he made a very important movie with two eminently decent people. Still, he was the one who had to bite his tongue and submit to the scrutiny of two nice but insensitive whites. The project moved ahead on the back of his self-suppression. And, in addition to any inner doubt this may have caused, he was also held in contempt by the black militants of the day for making the film at all. From the militant point of view, the movie showed a black man trying to convince a white man not to be racist. And when the white man finally forgoes his racism, the film becomes little more than an exercise in white self-congratulation. Iconic Negroes live in that territory between the doubt they feel (over the self-suppression they do in order to make things happen) and the charge from their own group that their success proves them to be sellouts. This tension is the price they pay for bringing a black presence fully into the American mainstream.

Of course, the music and films of today's rap and hip-hop culture are also quite successful in the American mainstream. But rap stars, no matter what their fame and fortune, do not become iconic Negroes. Rappers wear the challenger's mask, and their appeal—especially to the white youth who buy 80 percent of their CDs—is fundamentally subversive. They represent a convergence of adolescent rebellion and the black challenger's mask. So they offer up the black street life of gangs and drugs transformed into a theater of adolescent insolence tinged with black anger. Rappers like 50 Cent or Kanye West or Snoop Dogg make no offer of innocence to white America. They are utterly themselves—existential heroes, as their pose would have it—and whites must *earn* innocence by accepting them on their own terms. This is what makes them "bad," and, thus, the perfect embodiments of adolescent rebellion.

But rappers also can never be iconic Negroes because, as challengers, they don't dispel racial "otherness"; they wield it against whites. Like all challengers, they are racialists rather than humanists; they demand that tribute be paid to their race rather than to their humanity. So, they never elicit the kind of human identification and affection that Oprah elicits. They are always rebels within the kingdom.

Though a world away from rappers in sophistication, the post-sixties generation of black academics and intellectuals is also barred from iconic Negro status. They, too, are more challengers than bargainers, more racialists than humanists. Of course, there are many individual exceptions to this overview, but for the most part, black academics, journalists, and intellectuals have challenged their institutions for racial tribute—in the universities: racial preferences in hiring and student admissions, black studies programs, black "theme" dorms and cultural centers, black graduation ceremonies; in the newsroom: diversity hiring programs, race-sensitive language guidelines, special race "beats," the demand for minority management, and so on. And today, the prevailing dogma in American higher education (and to a lesser degree in American journalism) is the racialism of multiculturalism and diversity—both the fruit of relentless black and minority challenging over the last forty years.

Challenging has been an extremely fruitful mask for blacks in these areas. Universities, newspapers, magazines, educational and cultural foundations, even many corporations have literally tied their institutional legitimacy to evidence of their racial goodwill. They have reflexively rewarded even absurd black and minority challenges—racial "theme" dorms, "politically correct" language guidelines in news organizations—simply to make a show of that goodwill.

All of this was clear in the 2002 confrontation between Harvard University's president, Lawrence Summers, and the black Harvard professor Cornel West. When President Summers asked West to do more serious academic work—West had been away on the lucrative college speaking circuit and had even made a rap CD— it was Summers who ended up eating humble pie. Within days he was pressured into apologizing to West, who, in princely fashion, quickly vacated Harvard for Princeton, where, presumably, he would not be disturbed by such unseemly requests. The fact is that challenging has given blacks an autonomous—almost sovereign— authority within universities. It is arguably more important for the university to prove itself to blacks than it is for blacks to prove themselves to the university.

And yet, in the end, challengers can never win more than concessions. And the power they wield is so tied to their race that it tends to ghettoize them within institutions. It carves out minority tracks like "student services" and education departments within universities, or "human resources" within corporations. Challengers, unlike bargainers, ride on the back of their "otherness" rather than dispel it. *Difference* is their wedge and their power. So they have no positive bridge to the masses of Americans. And over time, they are easily seduced into believing more in themselves as blacks than as human beings.

Iconic Negroes, on the other hand, stand out as individuals, as black people whose racial pride is not exclusionary. It is true that they, too, wear a mask and that a certain discipline of self-suppression is required to stay within the contours of that mask. It is also true that the risk is on them when they make a gift of innocence and trust to whites, some of whom are clearly undeserving. But it is important to remember—given the shameful history of white supremacy—that there is nothing less than a profound, even ferocious, need in white America to dissociate from racism. This need, at its core, is a craving simply to be seen as decent against the cultural stigma that paints all whites as racists. In the pinch between this stigma and the simple need to feel decent there is enormous tension and energy. And this is precisely the energy that bargainers tap into when they offer whites "the benefit of the doubt." Their gesture of trust comes back in wave after wave of gratitude and goodwill. And this is what wraps people like Oprah in a special charisma, a beneficence that her white competitors can never have. She gives Americans their decency.

Iconic Negroes don't win many concessions from American institutions. But their willingness to see decency in the American people gives them a transformative power that challengers can never have. *The Cosby Show* gave Americans in New Mexico and Maine and Idaho a new way of seeing and thinking about black Americans. It did not solve the country's race problem, but it did nudge the culture in a positive direction. It was transformative.

# CHAPTER TEN

# Born to Bargain

Barack Obama is not only the first black American to plausibly run for the American presidency; he is the first to test the special charisma of the iconic Negro in national politics. Colin Powell clearly had iconic Negro status in the mid-nineties, and he might have been the first to test that status in the political arena, but in the end he demurred. So it has fallen to Obama to break this ground. Can an Oprahlike charisma translate into actual votes? We know it can sell things. And it has already taken a man only two years out of the Illinois state legislature and launched him into a serious bid for the presidency. But can it take him all the way? I often see "Oprah for President" bumper stickers—the gratitude factor given voice in political metaphor. But Obama will need more than metaphorical power.

Racially divided societies throw up iconic figures who seem to transcend the divide. And in America such figures always imply a very idealistic ideology of white absolution and black redemption—a perfectly ecumenical distribution of much-needed innocence. Oh, if only whites had no association with racism and if only blacks had no association with inferiority, then wouldn't the world be a better place? This is an ideological image— one to rally people behind—like the "classless society." But can it flutter down to earth and play a role in presidential politics?

Barack Obama is nothing if not an iconic Negro who is expressly identified with this ideology. It gives him his aura. And he must wonder at times where all the attention and affection come from. His wife, Michelle, often seems mystified by the waves of goodwill that wash over her husband, and she is given to making little deflating remarks about his household negligence that protest the idea of his specialness even as she campaigns for him. It would have to be intimidating to be married to someone who is suddenly numinous in the culture. Obama himself may not have set out to achieve this effect, but there it is, and he has to be much concerned now with how to sustain it. How to stay in that iconic territory where goodwill rolls right up to your front door?

One thing Obama instinctively knows is the art of bargaining. To this manner he seems to have been born.

In *Dreams from My Father* we see the high school senior Barack Obama *consciously* scheming to bargain with his own mother. A friend of his had been arrested for drug possession, and his mother "marched" into his room— obviously worried that he was involved in the same activity—and demanded the details of the arrest. Obama gave her "a reassuring smile and patted her hand and told her not to worry." This, he wrote, was "usually an effective tactic," because people "were satisfied so long as you were courteous and smiled and made no sudden moves. They were more than satisfied; they were relieved— such a pleasant surprise to find a well-mannered young black man who didn't seem angry all the time."

Well, there it was, the virtual definition of bargaining when he was no more than a senior in high school. There, already, was the gift of innocence—the "well-mannered young black man" trusting his mother not to disbelieve him, giving *her* the "benefit of the doubt" by implying that she was above doubting him. He, in his largesse, would endure her suspicions without *racial* anger, and she would be "relieved" at being spared that anger. (Obama himself acknowledged the use of this racial strategy with his mother.) And, in her relief, she would be grateful to him. She would overlook his likely involvement with drugs. Even the very young Barack Obama was something of an artist at bargaining. And if he was not secure in his black identity, he certainly knew white people. He knew how much they dreaded a truly angry confrontation with a black. Their worst fears could be realized in such confrontations. They could be smeared as racist with nothing behind them save their race's actual reputation for racism. History could convict them.

The only problem for the young Obama was that his mother didn't buy his bargaining. "She had just sat there, studying my eyes, her face as grim as a hearse." But, though his mother could not be bargained with, others clearly responded to the "well-mannered young black man who didn't seem angry all the time." Moreover, Barack Obama seems to have little talent for anger, which will always make the challenger's mask an awkward fit. Bargaining is his natural métier because he seems to understand it as a kind of charm—a charm that seizes on that first pleasant surprise that whites experience when they encounter a black who is not angry. How many times, growing up, would he have noticed that little surprise in whites? And how long would it have taken him to realize that it amounted to opportunity?

This is one of the ways the races condition each other. It is virtually Pavlovian. All my life, I have seen what Obama saw—that little pleasant reaction in whites at the absence of anger in blacks. Conditioning is inevitable with so consistent a stimulus. It happens organically in the flow of life, and whether one develops a talent for bargaining or challenging is largely an unconscious negotiation in which many factors come into play.

Challengers send out anger signals—coolness, a flat affect, an ambient hostility—that try to make whites *feel* white and, thus, defensive. Bargainers relieve the anxiety of being white. Of course, many blacks can be ambidextrous, but conditioning, temperament, and life possibilities usually combine to give us a leaning one way or the other. If one consciously uses the bargaining strategy, as the young Obama did with his mother, it is after the fact of already having *identified* with the bargaining mask.

So it was fate that made Barack Obama a natural bargainer. His interracial background, in itself, assuages considerable racial anxiety in whites. It makes the point that he is not likely to be angry at whites in some blanket way. After all, he was raised in a white family. His earliest and most formative human connections were with whites. So his very family background disarms him as a challenger, and gives whites that little grace note of surprise that relaxes them. As I have noted, the story of his interracial background is usually the first thing one hears about Obama. But it is also very often the first story he tells about himself.

At the 2004 Democratic Convention in Boston, Obama made the now famous speech that launched him as a new star in national politics. By the third sentence of that speech we had heard about his Kenyan father and grandfather, and by the eighth sentence we had met his white mother from Kansas. By the third paragraph we had the white grandparents as well as a reference to his parents' "improbable love." And then came a deft recasting of this pedigree that would have scandalized most Americans only a generation ago: "I stand here today, grateful for the diversity of my heritage." And ". . . in no other country on earth is my story even possible." Here, he both compliments his nation and gilds his "heritage" with today's golden word: "diversity."

But then, Obama had published *Dreams from My Father* almost a decade before this speech. In that small but interesting genre of interracial memoirs, this book will have a lasting place. Instead of the politician's usual guardedness, the book is almost naïve in its degree of self-disclosure. There are pretentious passages and longueurs, but there are also places where he writes as if the reader is almost beside the point, as if he is marching through certain emotional details for his own private purposes. The book will not be toted up as a political accomplishment, but it is an accomplishment nonetheless.

It goes too far to suggest that Obama's openness about his background in this book and in his speeches is conscious bargaining—that he is trying to manipulate America the way he tried to manipulate his mother back in high school. After all, he is a man with an unconventional background, and he no doubt hopes that that openness will make him more familiar to people. But this is also precisely what makes him a perfect bargainer. Apart from any intention on his part, his "heritage" does the most important thing a bargainer can do: it dispels racial otherness. It says to whites that he is not—and cannot be—the sort of black they fear, that menacing black "other" who would look upon their white skin as proof of racism.

In *Dreams,* he says, "Sometimes I would find myself talking to Ray [his black high school friend] about *white folks* this and *white folks* that, and I would suddenly remember my mother's smile, and the words I spoke would seem awkward and false. Or I would be helping Gramps dry the dishes after dinner and Toot [his grandmother] would come in to say she was going to sleep, and those same words—*white folks*—would flash in my head like a bright neon sign, and I would suddenly grow quiet, as if I had secrets to keep." *"White folks"* is a term that shames Obama. In his mouth, it is bigotry because it paints all whites with the same brush, and he knows in the most personal of ways that all whites are not the same. He knows that, where whites are concerned, he has to observe carefully, suspend judgment, and make distinctions. In other words, he has to give whites "the benefit of the doubt." He *has to* bargain. He *has to* give whites their innocence until they prove unworthy of it. This is what white Americans sense in Barack Obama. On pain of his own personal integrity, he simply cannot be a challenger.

Challengers—like Obama's black friend Ray—deprive whites of their racial innocence until they do something to earn it. They promote racial "otherness" because it is the basis of the identity politics that makes whites obligated and blacks entitled. They excite racial anxiety in whites rather than relieve it. Challenging is the mask worn so effectively by Al Sharpton, Jesse Jackson, and much of today's civil rights leadership—people and organizations surviving almost entirely on the money of American institutions on the run from the racist stigma. Such people are now grating annoyances in American life because they are opportunists living off the moral authority of black suffering.

Still, these all-too-familiar challengers have come to play an unexpected role in the Obama saga. It is precisely against the specter of an Al Sharpton that a Barack Obama looks so "fresh," "new," and "appealing." A figure like Sharpton literally *defines* Obama as a breath of fresh air. He is an advertisement *for* Obama—the overweight slattern next to the svelte beauty in the weight-loss ad. Sharpton and Jackson make the point—better than Obama's most savvy speechwriter ever could—that Obama is a black man for all people, a black man who *can only* give whites "the benefit of the doubt."

What white Americans deeply long for is a bargaining relationship with black America. Forty years of relentless challenging, of living under constant threat of stigmatization as a racist, of hearing that one's country is racist to the core, has generated a profound hunger in whites for bargaining—the chance simply to be given "the benefit of the doubt." It is Barack Obama's extraordinary good luck that the arc of his life and political career has intersected with this great hunger. He is a talented politician, but he is a phenomenon—an iconic Negro—because of this intersect.

Still, this blessing of luck is also what ultimately makes him a bound man. What the gods can give, they can take away.

# CHAPTER ELEVEN

# Bind I:
# The Discipline

As I walked past a newsstand the other day, Barack Obama's gravely serious face caught the corner of my eye. When I turned to look, there he was, all but glowering out from the cover of *Vanity Fair*. Instead of the familiar amiable Obama, it was a grave Obama of blunt frankness. There was challenge in his eyes, a little glare of anger. I thought it was a risky photograph for him. His charm was gone. He seemed almost ready to scold. This was not the look of a bargainer.

Then I stepped closer and saw the word "AFRICA" etched in huge translucent letters across the bottom half of the cover. The translucence of the letters—you could see the wrinkles in Obama's white shirt through them—made it easy to miss the word from a distance. But once the word "AFRICA" was in focus, Obama was instantly a bargainer again. (That entire issue of *Vanity Fair* was devoted to Africa.) In the context of modern Africa—the world's most tragic continent—a little glare of anger is hardly a challenge. He could have gotten away with more.

Discipline is the muscle that enables the masks of both bargaining and challenging to work. And before I understood the context of the photograph, it looked as if Obama's discipline might have lapsed—as if he had failed to keep at bay some impulse within himself to challenge. Discipline is simply the self-suppression that keeps out of sight those unruly parts of the self that might otherwise leap out and put the lie to the mask. When Obama is among only blacks, he might relax his discipline a bit and let a little challenging show. This is what he was doing in high school with his black friend Ray when he was throwing around the words *white folks.* The next day, in front of his English teacher or his white teammates on the basketball team, he would be the bargainer again, offering them the benefit of the doubt and suppressing his impulse to challenge.

Conversely, it is unimaginable that Al Sharpton would walk into a confrontation with a white authority figure—a police chief, a school official, a corporate CEO—and mention that racism had greatly declined in American life, though he might entertain this idea in the company of only blacks. These masks require great discipline because we are all far more varied and complex than the mask we wear. The barbershop is a cherished institution in every black community because no whites are present and one can be *undisciplined* without risk. The popular movie *Barbershop* stirred controversy because of a scene in which one of the barbers not only criticized Jesse Jackson but also said that O. J. Simpson was guilty—two statements that clearly violate the challenger's mask and would likely not be said in the presence of whites. There was controversy precisely because the movie was released for everyone to see. Both the movie *and* its release were breaches of discipline.

Again, the sole purpose of these masks is to enable blacks to gain things from the more powerful white majority by manipulating their need for racial innocence, and thus their sense of decency. If whites today—in what I've called the age of white guilt—didn't greatly need racial innocence in order to be decent people, there would be little market for bargaining and challenging. But whites *are* in fact stigmatized with past racism, and this does two things: it makes them a vast market for racial innocence and it gives blacks a monopoly over that innocence. So we blacks are ferociously disciplined around our two masks simply to protect this monopoly, to make sure that we keep our power over white innocence. We believe, as only a formerly oppressed people can believe, that our control over white innocence—our power to grant it or withhold it—is the greatest power we have in America.

And at the heart of this discipline there is one sacrosanct admonition: whether bargaining or challenging, you must never ever concede that only black responsibility can truly lift blacks into parity with whites. Black responsibility is verboten because it snuffs out the market for white innocence. If blacks should be responsible for their own uplift, then it is not racist for whites to expect them to do so. Black poverty and suffering are no longer automatically tied to white racism, because black uplift is dependent on what blacks do, not on what whites do. Now clear of the racist stigma, whites don't need to trade for their innocence with blacks. Whites can be racially moral people on their own terms. And we blacks then lose what we believed to be our greatest power in American life—our monopoly over white innocence, our power to set the terms of white decency.

So the first discipline of both bargainers and challengers is to deny in every way that black responsibility is by far the greatest—if not the only—transformative power available to blacks. Without this discipline, without the capacity to completely suppress this truth, both masks are defeated. If bargainers cannot vet whites with innocence, then there is no bargaining. And if challengers cannot withhold innocence from whites, then there is no leverage with which to challenge. If America accepts that blacks do in fact hold their fate in their own hands, then these masks simply evaporate.

And here is the pathos of American race relations. Obviously, black responsibility *is* the greatest—if not the only—transformative power available to blacks. How could it be otherwise? Just because we were oppressed, it does not follow that there is a force other than our own assumption of responsibility—our own agency—that will lift us up. Where in all of human history has one group been lifted up by the guilt or goodwill or need for innocence of another group? Where have former oppressors transformed their former victims?

And yet, black responsibility is the third rail of American race relations. If whites mention it, the stigma of racism falls upon them. If blacks mention it, they are Uncle Toms betraying their race by letting whites off the hook. Thus, we have so encircled this obvious truth with threats of stigmatization that it has become one of the most formidable taboos in American life.

Suppose Oprah Winfrey suddenly presented a series of programs making the point that individual responsibility was the greatest power available to black America. Suppose she argued that this was the only power that could truly enable blacks to overcome the myriad problems we face—the deterioration of the black family far past the point of crisis; an achievement gap that extends even into the black middle class; a black subculture of gangs, drugs, and violence; a 70 percent illegitimacy rate; and so on. Suppose she announced that racism, while still a nuisance, had receded to the point where individual responsibility could at last pay off for blacks and could now become the main engine of group advancement. She might offer the caveat that others could be helpful but only if they never took over responsibility from blacks. She could also say that America owed blacks scrupulous fairness, freedom from discrimination, and equal treatment under the law. But then, to reinforce her main theme, suppose she said that we blacks—like free peoples everywhere—should be *entirely* responsible for our uplift whether or not help or even fairness came from others. After all, it was our assumption of responsibility that made the civil rights movement successful. What would be the likely consequence for Oprah Winfrey, one of the great bargainers of all time, were she to go down this road?

She would lose her status as an iconic Negro. An insistence on black responsibility is not a feature of the bargainer's mask. It offers no innocence to whites, no benefit of the doubt. It doesn't flatter them or give them an opportunity to experience their own decency against their race's reputation for racism. It asks for no gratitude. By definition, black responsibility is a *disengagement* from the idea that whites are crucial to black uplift. In this way, it abandons whites in their longing for racial innocence and restored moral authority. It leaves them, as it were, to flap in the breeze. And in this circumstance they would have no reason to imbue Oprah with a special allure.

Worse, by advocating for black responsibility, Oprah would be taking a stand that stigmatizes whites as racist. Whites cannot simply demand that blacks take responsibility for their own problems without coming off as victim-blaming racists. In other words, if whites followed Oprah in her commitment to black responsibility, they would *lose* innocence rather than gain it. Suddenly, Oprah would be a liability, a weight, a barrier to their innocence.

So, then, that wonderful reciprocity that bargainers have with whites would break down. There would be no synergy, no escalation of gratitude and goodwill. A strong and clear commitment to black responsibility would likely not cause Oprah to become a despised figure. However, she would be shorn of that extra-specialness that bargaining generates. Given her talent and charm, she would no doubt still be quite successful. But iconic status would elude her.

Pretty much all of this has happened—in reality—to the great comedian Bill Cosby. Once every bit the iconic Negro that Oprah is today, Cosby in recent years has

made the argument for black responsibility more promi-
nently than anyone since—yes—Malcolm X, who was a
fierce advocate of black self-help back in the sixties.
Cosby presses for the self-help without the black nationalism, and he travels from city to city staging "call-outs"
in which he challenges inner-city blacks to take charge of
their families and to raise their children with values and
purpose. In Cincinnati, to make his point, he had the
local coroner—a black doctor—come on stage to
describe in graphic detail what happens to a human body
when it is shot. On television we see such bodies dis-
creetly covered with a tarpaulin. But the coroner
describes to the audience what he finds when he removes
that tarpaulin and examines the actual body. In the
course of description his own emotions break through.
His eyes water as he describes finding one young black
male after another under those tarpaulins.

Cosby brings on stage the mothers of teenagers
killed in the endless roundelay of gang violence. He
brings up people who suffered sexual abuse as children,
people who lost themselves to drugs, and girls who all
but destroyed their lives with teenage pregnancies. He
asks people to tell their story, to "testify," and to describe
to the audience how they stood up to these problems.
Underlying this combination of shock therapy and tes-
timony is the theme of individual responsibility. But it is
not something that has to be preached. He believes that

the people who face up to their problems and make progress against them are the best "experts" and teachers.

Well, Bill Cosby is no doubt doing God's work in all of this, but it has cost him. Clearly, this effort breaks the discipline of the bargainer's mask that gave him iconic status in his *Cosby Show* days. This work represents a disengagement from the idea of black uplift through white guilt. So it leaves him no way to offer innocence or flattery to whites, or to receive gratitude from them. And whites cannot follow him in this focus on black individual responsibility without risking the racist stigma. So he is now something of a liability even to whites who privately admire his "call-outs" and who were proud to be fans of the *Cosby Show*. He is now a risk to their innocence rather than a source of it.

Cosby is still one of the greatest comedians of his time, and people will always pay to see him perform. But he broke discipline with the bargainer's mask by revealing himself to be a deeper and stronger man than the brilliant bargainer we had always known. This disrupted the easy reciprocity he once had with the American public. He is no longer an iconic Negro. He no longer sells Jell-O, or anything else, on national television.

Bill Cosby gave up his iconic status to be free of the disciplines of bargaining, to speak as he truly felt without regard to his reciprocity with white America. (He literally said at an NAACP meeting, "I don't care what white people think"—thereby removing his mask in public.) The first binding reality for Barack Obama is that his political cachet is tied to his status as an iconic Negro. If he goes the way of Cosby, he loses actual political capital. He might well survive such a move, but the "rock star" specialness would be gone. *White Americans would no longer see the possibility of their own racial innocence in him.*

So the disciplines of bargaining are a basic element of Obama's politics. He labors to sell himself as an "optimistic sign from the racial front," as the harbinger of a new America in which old divisions of ideology and race are transcended. Here—against the shame of America's racial past—he may hope to look a bit messianic. As one fan put it at a recent rally in Reno, Nevada, he is "the guy America is waiting for." So you don't vote for Obama merely because of his policy positions on health care and school subsidies; he is an opportunity to vote for American redemption.

Bargainers nurture a degree of invisibility about themselves because they want nothing visible that could break off their reciprocity with whites. Oprah may occasionally endorse a candidate (she endorses Obama) but she does not spell out her political convictions, and she certainly does not belabor them as Phil Donahue once did. Iconic Negroes try for political invisibility and, failing this, they lean vaguely toward the political left.

Why? Because on the political left blacks are still seen as victims.

If blacks are not victims of white racism, if their problems stem from pathologies only remotely related to past racism—if, in fact, more black responsibility is the only meaningful answer to black difficulty—then whites begin to disengage from the idea that their solicitude brings black advancement. Suddenly, they don't need so much of the innocence that bargainers offer them. So bargainers lean toward the political left, where the focus is on white responsibility for black difficulty.

Barack Obama is bound to the *anti*responsibility political left because his political fate depends on his ability to offer innocence to whites—this despite the fact that he clearly seems to accept the importance of individual responsibility in social reform. For his own mother, apparently, responsibility was a rigid creed. He says of her, "The idea that my survival depended on luck remained a heresy to her; she insisted on assigning responsibility. . . ." Yet he offers no thinking on how to build incentives to responsibility into actual social policy.

The scenarios he paints to justify his broad policy directions always return us to the idea of the victim. He thinks of the many fatherless young black males on the South Side of Chicago and sees their "last best hope" in school reform. Clearly, the schools these boys attend are little better than holding pens. But isn't the larger problem the fact that they come from a subculture—

generated in good measure by post-sixties welfare policies—in which nothing serious or difficult is asked of
anyone? Nothing. Mothers are not asked to raise their
children within a framework of values and expectations
that might prepare them to succeed in school. Fathers are
not expected to be fathers in any sense of the word
beyond procreation itself. And the schools themselves—
black schools staffed by black teachers and administra-
tors—are not expected to truly educate. The teachers in
these schools famously send their own children to private
schools. In a world where nothing is asked of anyone,
where there is in fact a stunning *rejection* of responsibility, what good is yet another round of school reform?

But if Barack Obama crossed the road, so to speak,
away from what government systems can do, and began
to talk about individual responsibility as the purest and
most immediate form of social power available to the
poor, he would surely suffer Bill Cosby's fate. And so he
is a bound man. He cannot be himself without hurting
himself politically. His mother's humble and clear idea of
responsibility—which served him so well—would put his
political fortunes at risk were he to adopt it. Here there
must be a nasty wrestling of the self back into the bargainer's mask. Find a way around your mother's truth.
Disregard evidence from your own experience. Learn to
see poor blacks as unsalvageable but for white rescue.
Learn the intellectual circumlocutions that take you

through black responsibility and safely back to black victimization.

So Obama is not given to "fresh" or "new" ideas. It is
hard to be an iconic Negro and original at the same time.
He works within convention, not against it. When you
are an iconic Negro, *you* are original, not your thinking.
You have taken the bargainer's discipline and fashioned
*yourself,* not your thought. In fact, you have thoughts to
touch everyone's base, thoughts that recognize and flatter everyone. But you have few *visible* convictions.

When you are iconic, and bound therein, you have
no mandate upon which to run for the presidency
beyond the offering of yourself.

# CHAPTER TWELVE

# Bind II:
# Is He Black Enough?

White people like Barack Obama a little too much for the comfort of many blacks. How is it possible, the suspicion goes, to stir that much excitement and affection in whites, to become a darling of the mainstream left, and still be loyal to one's own people? Blacks instinctively know that Obama is a bargainer. In other words, we blacks know that Obama is out there—and not in the arts or entertainment but in the political arena—*giving whites the benefit of the doubt.* He is granting them racial innocence before they give him anything. We see, too, that they are flattered by the trust he has placed in them and grateful that he risks his political fortunes on the expectation that they will be decent. We see that Obama has worked up a reciprocity with whites and turned it into political capital.

This is something new. No black before Obama has employed the bargainer's charms in pursuit of so high an office. We are used to black challengers, like Jesse Jackson and Al Sharpton, who chase the well-lit platform of a presidential candidacy for many reasons, though actually winning even the Democratic nomination is not one of them. Jackson's 1984 bid for the Democratic nomination was respectable only because it was so improbable. Life-long protesters are not likely to have developed an easy reciprocity with white voters. On the other hand, no one ever asks them if they are black enough.

And this points to the fundamental impossibility that binds Barack Obama. He exploded onto the American political scene precisely because he is a bargainer and *not* a challenger—a black adept at getting whites to see their own racial innocence in him. But this same genius for bargaining makes him a suspicious figure—"not black enough"—to blacks. To make matters worse, as a Democrat he must have *both* the white and black Democratic vote to do well in the primaries as well as in the general election, assuming he gets that far.

If, to please blacks, Obama does more challenging, he begins to lose his iconic status with whites, his ability to flatter them with trust. He loses white votes because whites don't want a challenging Al Sharpton; they want the iconic Negro, the bargainer in whom they see their own innocence and the nation's redemption. If, to please whites, Obama bargains more, trades more innocence to whites, he loses votes among blacks—a vital constituency in the Democratic party—who define blackness as challenging, as withholding innocence from whites.

Since the sixties, the black American identity has been broadly and deeply defined by challenging—an almost nationalistic idea of one's racial self with overtones of separatism. And this is especially so in the realm of politics, where real power is contested. Black Americans have been willing, with some reservations, to accept black bargainers in fields outside politics—entertainment, sports, television. But even so, every black who becomes iconic catches a degree of hell from other blacks. Oprah Winfrey, Bill Cosby, Colin Powell, Tiger Woods, and Michael Jordan have all been accused of not being black enough. (Interestingly, if iconic Negroes get into serious trouble, as O. J. Simpson and Michael Jackson have, they magically become black again as blacks rally to them to keep the race's reputation from being besmirched.) But most iconic Negroes function far outside the arena of electoral politics. Obama is the first black to bargain his way to national *political* importance and, as such, he is far more threatening to today's black identity than other iconic Negroes.

Consequently, it is his odd fate to threaten the identity of the group from which he needs almost unanimous support to be politically viable. And here his interracial background is not helpful, since it makes challenging—blackness itself—very difficult. Challengers have to blanketly assess whites to effectively hold their innocence hostage. They lose leverage if they start making distinctions, seeing some whites as better than others. Obama's background forces him to make such distinctions. At the very least, he will have a nuanced view of whites, and blacks will sense that this weakens him as a challenger.

So to curry the black vote, Obama from time to time tries on the challenger's mask. His speech in Selma, Alabama, marking the anniversary of the famous voting rights march across the Edmund Pettus Bridge, was before a black audience composed of civil rights veterans, challengers all. In a black-inflected accent that he never uses elsewhere, Obama put a challenger's spin on his background. "My very existence might not have been possible had it not been for some of the people here today. So don't tell me I don't have a claim on Selma, Alabama. Don't tell me I'm not coming home to Selma, Alabama." Several weeks later, Obama appeared at a meeting of Rev. Al Sharpton's National Action Network and again donned the challenger's mask. "These aren't issues [civil rights] that are new to me. These aren't issues that I just decided to start talking about as a presidential candidate. They are the causes of my life." Just a few days later, however, at the largely white California Democratic Convention, he was the perfect bargainer again. "I learned that . . . you can turn the page on

old debates . . . we can assume the best in people instead
of the worst."

With blacks he is a protester carrying forward the
race's cause; with whites he is the "one people" unifier,
minimizing the importance of racial difference—even
suggesting that blacks are best helped by government
policies that are not race-specific. But the point is not
that Obama is a hypocrite. Hillary Clinton shamelessly
breaks into imitations of the black vernacular that sound
like the squeak of chalk on a blackboard every time she
appears before a black audience. The point is that, in politics, when the matter of race is in play—and it is always
in play with a black candidate—the entire history of
black-white relations in America comes forward, after
centuries of convoluted evolution, and makes itself felt
in its most recent configuration. So if Obama seems the
hypocrite, it is also true that he is only working within
the world that he finds, within a configuration of forces
much larger than himself.

And what makes today's configuration so powerful is
that it defines our racial identities. For example, challenging now defines the black American identity because
whites are now contrite over their historic association
with white supremacy. Blacks are challengers today
because whites have *responded* to challenging. And whites
have responded because they long for the racial innocence that their association with historic racism denies
them. This is only the most recent configuration in the

long evolution of American race relations—*an evolution throughout which neither race could ever fully know itself except in relation to the other.*

Today, both blacks and whites see Barack Obama's presidential bid as potentially a new signal from history. He makes whites hopeful for a new racial configuration in which they might get more benefit of the doubt; he makes blacks (though primarily the black leadership) anxious at this same prospect. Already, his bright success as a bargainer suggests that white America may be sending a signal of its own: that it is exhausted from forty years of being challenged and is therefore doubly grateful to blacks who approach with at least some faith in the fundamental decency of whites.

And yet, apart from whatever he may portend, Obama is today a bound man who cannot serve the aspirations of one race without betraying those of the other. It is easy to have the impression, given all the excitement that attends him, that he is, as they say, "fresh," "new," and unconventional. But in many ways his truest problem—the reason he is bound—is exactly that he is so utterly conventional. Barack Obama works entirely within the current configuration of race relations—the masks of bargaining and challenging, the need in whites for racial innocence. And he exploits that world to move *himself* ahead, not to advance a new configuration of race relations—or to end such configurations altogether. He is neither a revolutionary nor even a reformist. He is simply infatuated with the possibilities of his own skin color *within the world as it is,* not as it should or could be. His genius is to know his currency *within* the status quo.

What is exceptional about Barack Obama is the same thing that was exceptional about Louis Armstrong. Neither man discovered a new way for society to racially arrange itself. But both men found a way to capture the goodwill of whites in a way that facilitated their lives and careers. If Obama has considerable political talent just as Armstrong had musical genius, both men in the end were racial pragmatists.

But bargainers who become iconic Negroes always experience a pushback from their own people. As an entertainer, Armstrong could find his way through this. But Obama needs the votes of the people who would push back against him. And to halt this resistance, he has to wear the challenger's mask that whites—his primary supporters—hate. In the end, he is bound by the same racial configuration that he has exploited.

# CHAPTER THIRTEEN

# "The Visible Man"

Can a black ask for power at the level of the American presidency without wearing a mask, without reassuring whites that they will be given the benefit of the doubt—without lessoning the anxiety inherent in being white today? Is real power possible for blacks without some negotiation with white innocence? And what would a black who was neither a challenger nor a bargainer look like?

Perhaps the most troubling character in the rich gallery of characters in Ralph Ellison's masterpiece, *Invisible Man,* is Tod Clifton—a tall, articulate, and dark-skinned young man with the sort of special appeal that makes him a natural leader and the envy of the invisible man, the novel's young black protagonist. Clifton is a survivor of the ideological warfare between the Brotherhood (the metaphorical communists) and the black nationalists in the Harlem of the 1940s. When the invisible man meets Clifton, he has become—by dint of his talent and charisma—an important leader in the Brotherhood. Clifton is far more experienced than the invisible man at negotiating the mix of rigid personalities and rigid ideas that compose the Brotherhood. In this largely white world, he is masterly where the invisible man is uncertain and awkward.

Then the inexplicable happens. Clifton abruptly quits the Brotherhood and disappears. Then the invisible man spots him racially debasing himself by selling black Sambo dolls on the streets of New York. Finally, a few months after leaving the Brotherhood, Clifton is shot and killed by a white policeman under mysterious circumstances. Shocked and numbed by so swift a demise, the invisible man suddenly sees Clifton as a cautionary tale. Naïvely, he tells himself that he is lucky still to be in the Brotherhood, and then he asks himself one of the novel's most profound questions: "Why would a man deliberately plunge outside of history?"

Ellison is working here on the level of allegory, and he uses Clifton's story to represent a dilemma central to the black American experience. In order to be a part of history, to participate in its relentless evolution, the black American has always had to don the mask that would enable him to join the larger white world, where, presumably, history is being made. Thus, to a degree, inauthenticity has been the price blacks have paid to join history. Clifton did well in the Brotherhood by making himself into someone he wasn't. And finally, this sense of inauthenticity caught up to him. He took off the mask. He dropped out of the Brotherhood—this symbolic communist organization that literally defined its mission as the creation of a new history for man. Thus, the price for acting in the interest of his own authenticity—for being maskless—was to fall outside of history.

And here Ellison drew a sharp contrast between the white world of unfolding history and the black world of chaos that Clifton fell into. If there was inauthenticity for blacks inside the white world, it did not follow that there was authenticity inside the black world. As Ellison represented it, the black world was an existential chaos where no meaning was firm and where history was forgotten as soon as it was made. There was nothing solid upon which to build an authentic self. When Clifton fell out of white history, he did not find his true self; he fell to pieces. Here was a man who had sacrificed so much for the dignity of his race, selling Sambo dolls to racist white people. He had descended into a black world so bereft of meaning that self-abasement had become the same thing as dignity.

As the invisible man sat meditating on Clifton, he spotted a group of young blacks who eerily foreshadow today's gangbangers and rappers. They were loud, colorful, and completely self-invented out of the ahistorical chaos of black life. They were existential cowboys wearing no mask for the white world, and yet, for all their self-satisfaction, they were completely outside of history.

Perhaps Ellison's demarcation of the black dilemma—a choice between inauthenticity and chaos—is too severe for the current age. Today, rap music is a multibillion-dollar industry. The existential cowboys, for better or for worse, have come inside history. Today, there is a large black middle class that goes to work each day in every imaginable American institution. And many of its members would be appalled to think that they wear a racial mask, or that they enter and leave history as if through a turnstile. Certainly, the civil rights victories of the sixties, and the great social transformations that followed, make it difficult for black Americans today to think of themselves as dwelling outside of history.

Nonetheless, Barack Obama *entered* history by wearing the bargainer's mask. He was born to a fate that literally schooled him in bargaining. It was not a hard-earned and carefully evolved individuality that won him entrée into the national imagination. It was the matching of his racial *persona* with a hunger for racial innocence in white America. Here he was like Tod Clifton in the Brotherhood, a man with a skill for becoming well regarded among whites. And this skill, this facility, has already taken Obama far. It is almost impossible not to confuse this talent with actual character—not to presume that the warmth he elicits from whites is a response to his character rather than to his mask. But this is how Clifton finally lost himself: he had entered history but he wasn't anybody. He had success but no self.

What gave Barack Obama the idea that he could *plausibly* run for the presidency of the United States? Was it that he had evolved a compelling vision for the nation grounded in deeply held personal convictions? Or was it that he had simply become aware of his power to enthrall whites?

If—as Tod Clifton discovered—the mask is history's price of admission for blacks, then this is a pressure to make inauthenticity into a talent, to keep fashioning and adapting a racial persona rather than becoming the individual who is only black among many other things. And it was masking, not convictions, that brought Barack Obama forward in American life. He is decidedly not a conviction politician. His supporters do not look to him to *do* something; they look to him primarily to *be* something, to *represent* something. He is a bound man because he cannot *be* two opposing worldviews at the same time—he cannot grant whites their racial innocence and simultaneously withhold it from them.

Barack Obama emerged into a political culture that needed him more as an icon than as a man. He has gone far because the need is great. But this easy appeal has also been his downfall. It is a seduction away from character and conviction. In the Brotherhood, Tod Clifton thought he never had to discover what *he* truly believed. He never considered his true self to be relevant. When he finally lurches away from this falseness, there is no self to guide him toward a meaningful life. Probably the greatest debilitation in black American life is that our history of masking—once so necessary to our survival—has caused us to overvalue the manipulation of white people and to undervalue the evolution of our individual selves.

The challenge for Barack Obama is the same as it is for all free people: to achieve *visibility* as an individual, to in fact become an individual rather than a racial cipher. Today, he is in the same peril of falling "out of history" as the fictional Tod Clifton was sixty years ago. Unless we get to know who he is—what beliefs he would risk his life for—he could become a cautionary tale in his own right, an iconic figure who neglected to become himself.

# INDEX

Iconic Negro (*cont.*)
  political invisibility of,
    116–17, 123
  pushback of blacks against,
    127
  self-suppression of, 90–91
  sense of otherness dispelled
    by, 89–90
Idealization
  of absent father, 21
  of black identity, 26–27
Identification, gestures of, 37,
  38
Identity politics, 8, 29–31, 42,
  51–52, 69
  otherness as basis for,
    103–4
Illegitimacy rates, 71, 112
Illinois state legislature, 12
Imus, Don, 78–79
Indonesia, Obama's childhood
  in, 17, 39–40, 52
*In the Heat of the Night*
  (movie), 84
Innocence, racial, 61–62, 64,
  92, 129, 133
  bargain for, 74–77,
    82–86, 94–95, 99, 103,
    121
  black responsibility versus,
    113, 115, 116
  dispensation by challengers
    of, 77–80, 125

manipulation of need for,
  109–10
Integration, post-World
  War II, 63
Intellectuals, black, 92–94
Interracial background, 3–8,
  101–2, 123–24
  black identity and, 26–31
  vulnerability due to, 5–7
Interracial marriage, 49–51,
  81–83
*Invisible Man, The* (Ellison),
  129–34

Jackson, Jesse, 8, 85, 104, 109,
  122
Jackson, Michael, 123
Jazz, 59–65, 89
Jefferson, Thomas, 46
Jim Crow segregation, 60–61
Jordan, Michael, 89, 123
Journalism, challengers in,
  92–93

King, Martin Luther, Jr., 8, 26,
  27
Kroft, Steve, 6

Language, race-sensitive,
  92–93
Liberalism, 52
Literature, search for father in,
  18–21

# ABOUT THE AUTHOR

Shelby Steele is the Robert J. and Marion E. Oster Senior Fellow at the Hoover Institution (Stanford University), specializing in the study of race in democratic societies, multiculturalism, and Americn political culture. A recipient of the Bradley Prize, the National Humanities Medal, the National Book Critics' Award (for *The Content of Our Character: A New Vision of Race in America*), and an Emmy Award for television writing, Steele has written extensively for major publications including *The New York Times* and *The Wall Street Journal*. He is a contributing editor at *Harper's* magazine.

Steele is the author of *White Guilt: How Blacks and Whites Together Destroyed the Promise of the Civil Rights Era; A Dream Deferred: The Second Betrayal of Black Freedom in America;* and *The Content of Our Character: A New Vision of Race in America*.